SpringerBriefs in Applied Sciences and Technology

SpringerBriefs present concise summaries of cutting-edge research and practical applications across a wide spectrum of fields. Featuring compact volumes of 50 to 125 pages, the series covers a range of content from professional to academic.

Typical publications can be:

- A timely report of state-of-the art methods
- An introduction to or a manual for the application of mathematical or computer techniques
- A bridge between new research results, as published in journal articles
- A snapshot of a hot or emerging topic
- An in-depth case study
- A presentation of core concepts that students must understand in order to make independent contributions

SpringerBriefs are characterized by fast, global electronic dissemination, standard publishing contracts, standardized manuscript preparation and formatting guidelines, and expedited production schedules.

On the one hand, **SpringerBriefs in Applied Sciences and Technology** are devoted to the publication of fundamentals and applications within the different classical engineering disciplines as well as in interdisciplinary fields that recently emerged between these areas. On the other hand, as the boundary separating fundamental research and applied technology is more and more dissolving, this series is particularly open to trans-disciplinary topics between fundamental science and engineering.

Indexed by EI-Compendex, SCOPUS and Springerlink.

Daniele Spoladore · Elena Pessot · Marco Sacco
Editors

Digital and Strategic Innovation for Alpine Health Tourism

Natural Resources, Digital Tools and Innovation Practices from HEALPS 2 Project

Editors
Daniele Spoladore
Institute of Intelligent Industrial
Technologies and Systems for Advanced
Manufacturing (STIIMA), National
Research Council of Italy (CNR)
Lecco, Italy

Elena Pessot
Institute of Intelligent Industrial
Technologies and Systems for Advanced
Manufacturing (STIIMA), National
Research Council of Italy (CNR)
Lecco, Italy

Marco Sacco
Institute of Intelligent Industrial
Technologies and Systems for Advanced
Manufacturing (STIIMA), National
Research Council of Italy (CNR)
Lecco, Italy

ISSN 2191-530X   ISSN 2191-5318 (electronic)
SpringerBriefs in Applied Sciences and Technology
ISBN 978-3-031-15456-0   ISBN 978-3-031-15457-7 (eBook)
https://doi.org/10.1007/978-3-031-15457-7

© The Editor(s) (if applicable) and The Author(s) 2023. This book is an open access publication.
Open Access This book is licensed under the terms of the Creative Commons Attribution 4.0 International License (http://creativecommons.org/licenses/by/4.0/), which permits use, sharing, adaptation, distribution and reproduction in any medium or format, as long as you give appropriate credit to the original author(s) and the source, provide a link to the Creative Commons license and indicate if changes were made.
The images or other third party material in this book are included in the book's Creative Commons license, unless indicated otherwise in a credit line to the material. If material is not included in the book's Creative Commons license and your intended use is not permitted by statutory regulation or exceeds the permitted use, you will need to obtain permission directly from the copyright holder.
The use of general descriptive names, registered names, trademarks, service marks, etc. in this publication does not imply, even in the absence of a specific statement, that such names are exempt from the relevant protective laws and regulations and therefore free for general use.
The publisher, the authors, and the editors are safe to assume that the advice and information in this book are believed to be true and accurate at the date of publication. Neither the publisher nor the authors or the editors give a warranty, expressed or implied, with respect to the material contained herein or for any errors or omissions that may have been made. The publisher remains neutral with regard to jurisdictional claims in published maps and institutional affiliations.

This Springer imprint is published by the registered company Springer Nature Switzerland AG
The registered company address is: Gewerbestrasse 11, 6330 Cham, Switzerland

Preface

Alpine regions are characterized by exceptional natural resources, cultural heritage, healthy climate, and long tourism tradition. Tourism is a major component of economic growth, with several employment opportunities, and of great importance for the Alpine regions, with many positive effects on the local and regional population.

Natural resources can determine the development of competitive tourism destinations and drive the development of nature-based value chains aimed at enhancing tourists' health and well-being. Historically, the small size of most enterprises, the difficulties in establishing collaborative relationships between industry operators, and the lack of strategic projects aimed at the use and exploitation of natural resources, have hindered a systematic development of a nature-based health tourism (NHT) value chain. Nowadays, tourist market segments are changing the industry competitiveness with the request for more nature-based experiential programs, integrating both rewarding elements of beauty, relaxation, and regeneration, and more demanding elements such as preventative activities and sports. There is an increasing consciousness of the importance of local environmental and cultural preservation, the search for relax and stress-relieving products, and the overall authenticity of the vacation experience. Beyond lifestyle changes, key trends reshaping the health tourism landscape in Alpine regions include population ageing, climate change, and consequences of the COVID-19 pandemic both in terms of business losses and the need for natural remedies against these virus's long-term effects.

This background challenges health tourism operators to rethink the industry dynamics with a more innovation-driven strategy and business development, as well as facilitation of transnational cooperation among all kinds of actors. These include sectoral and specialized agencies such as destination management organizations, business support organizations, and tourism organizations; regional councils and municipalities in charge of policy-making and tourism strategy development; tourism facilities and companies (especially small- and medium-sized enterprises); universities and research centres that conduct applied research and development within the health tourism sector and related sectors, based on natural resources or health-related issues; interest groups and networks supporting nature-based and sustainable health tourism. Despite the richness of natural resources and health-promoting activities that spread among Alpine regions, the NHT landscape is characterized by innovation spatial fragmentation, lack of access to knowledge, and little transversal cooperation for value creation and sharing.

Aimed to address these key territorial challenges, the HEALPS2 project "Healing Alps: Tourism based on natural health resources as strategic innovation for the development of Alpine regions" was funded in the Priority "Innovative Alpine Space" of the Interreg Alpine Space program. The key objective of the project was to improve the framework conditions for utilizing the Alpine natural health resources by leveraging existing and newly developed NHT products and service chains to enhance access to knowledge and sharing of experiences at a transnational level. The main project activities took place from October 2019 to June 2022 and involved 11 organizations from 6 countries, i.e. Austria, Italy, Slovenia, Germany, France, and Switzerland. The collaboration between the project partners led to the development of a set of innovation practices and digital solutions, properly combined with the latest research results in tourism and health-related issues and the requirements of health tourism stakeholders collected in several events organized at the local and regional level. The vision of the project is to contribute to the positioning of the Alpine Space as a globally attractive health-promoting place, with a virtuous process of value generation and sharing among Alpine assets, actors, and territories.

This book incorporates the key knowledge and experiences, in terms of concepts, tools, and practices, developed within the HEALPS2 project, here organized into eight chapters. The content was purposefully organized to dedicate to the core assets for an Alpine NHT industry excellence, i.e. the natural resources and their healing effects; the digital tools enhancing the collection, advanced analytics and spread of data on NHT industry for supporting strategic decision-making; the innovation practices and communication strategies to properly engage the industry stakeholders.

Chapter One "Medical Evidence of Alpine Natural Resources as a Base for Health Tourism", Chapter Two "KPI for Data-Driven Assessment of Innovative Development Paths for Nature-Based Health Tourism in the Alpine Region", and Chapter Three "Alpine Assets, Perceptions and Strategies for Nature-Based Health Tourism" focus on the linkages between tourism, natural resources, and healing effects, with the identification and analysis of health benefits of Alpine resources and best practices, and related key performance indicators and perceptions by suppliers and tourists. These three initial chapters address scholars in the fields of health tourism and ecomedicine, but they also aim to inform tourism destination managers and policymakers on the foundational concepts to develop an NHT offer and enrich existing products based on local natural resources.

The following chapters present the digital tools implemented in the project, specifically Chapter Four "An Ontology-Based Decision Support System to Foster Innovation and Competitiveness Opportunities of Health Tourism Destinations" and Chapter Five "A Digital Application for Strategic Development of Health Tourism Destinations". These two chapters are mainly dedicated to developers and researchers in semantic Web technologies, with implementations in the health tourism sector. The developed tools are devoted to supporting NHT stakeholders such as sectoral and specialized agencies (destination management organizations, business support organizations, tourism organizations) and regional councils and municipalities, in the systematic sharing of knowledge for tourism strategy development and decision-making.

The final chapters are dedicated to transversal strategies and practices to support the proper exploitation of natural resources, use of digital tools, and spread of knowledge in the nature-based health tourism industry. Chapter Six presents "A Methodology for Participatory Stakeholder Engagement in Nature-Based Health Tourism", Chapter Seven focuses on "Innovation Practices and Techniques for Nature-Based Health Tourism Competitiveness", and finally Chapter Eight is dedicated to the "Strategic Communication in a Transnational Project—The Interreg Alpine Space Project HEALPS2". These chapters provide useful insights from HEALPS2 results for all NHT stakeholders who would invest to further unleash NHT industry innovation and collaboration opportunities in the Alpine regions.

Finally, the conclusions report an overview of the findings of the book and open up further research and application opportunities.

European Regional Development Fund

Lecco, Italy	Daniele Spoladore
Lecco, Italy	Elena Pessot
Lecco, Italy	Marco Sacco
Salzburg, Austria	Arnulf J. Hartl
Salzburg, Austria	Christina Pichler
Salzburg, Austria	Michael Bischof

Contents

Medical Evidence of Alpine Natural Resources as a Base for Health Tourism 1
Christina Pichler, Arnulf J. Hartl, Renate Weisböck-Erdheim, and Michael Bischof

KPI for Data-Driven Assessment of Innovative Development Paths for Nature-Based Health Tourism in the Alpine Region 31
Michael Bischof and Arnulf J. Hartl

Alpine Assets, Perceptions and Strategies for Nature-Based Health Tourism 49
Jan Mosedale, Arnulf Hartl, Christina Pichler, and Michael Bischof

An Ontology-Based Decision Support System to Foster Innovation and Competitiveness Opportunities of Health Tourism Destinations 61
Daniele Spoladore and Elena Pessot

A Digital Application for Strategic Development of Health Tourism Destinations 73
Atieh Mahroo, Daniele Spoladore, Paolo Ferrandi, and Ilenia Lovato

A Methodology for Participatory Stakeholder Engagement in Nature-Based Health Tourism 87
Danilo Čeh, Mirjana Nenad, and Elena Pessot

Innovation Practices and Techniques for Nature-Based Health Tourism Competitiveness 99
Mirjana Nenad and Elena Pessot

Strategic Communication in a Transnational Project—The Interreg Alpine Space Project HEALPS2 117
Daniele Spoladore, Marta Geri, and Veronika Widmann

Conclusion 129

Medical Evidence of Alpine Natural Resources as a Base for Health Tourism

Christina Pichler, **Arnulf J. Hartl**, **Renate Weisböck-Erdheim, and Michael Bischof**

Abstract The Alpine space disposes of excellent prerequisites to respond to the increasing demand of nature-based health tourism. Despite a growing scientific knowledge on the manifold benefits of human interaction with Alpine natural resources, the health tourism potential has not yet been fully exploited by Alpine regions. Based on major push and pull factors, the current state of scientific knowledge on the healing potential of nine selected natural Alpine resources is presented and discussed with regard to their health tourism potential. Major research gaps as well as starting points for future studies are demonstrated. In this way, the present work contributes to an applicable knowledge base on the health benefits of Alpine resources to enhance regional innovation capacity in terms of sustainable health tourism development. As tourism regions are increasingly taking evidence-based approaches to health tourism and regional development, the resulting lighthouses will contribute to the positioning of the Alpine space as globally attractive healing environment.

Keywords Alpine natural resources · Nature-based tourism · Evidence-based health tourism · Sustainable regional development · Alpine healing potential · Healing environment

1 Introduction

Outdoor recreation in natural environments is increasingly recognized as important for improving human health and well-being, especially in urbanized societies with diminished possibilities for human contact with nature [1–3]. The global COVID-19 pandemic has further highlighted the enormous value of engaging with nature and the strong need for a mutually advantageous relationship between humans and the natural environment [4].

C. Pichler (✉) · A. J. Hartl · R. Weisböck-Erdheim · M. Bischof
Institute of Ecomedicine, Paracelsus Medical University Salzburg, Salzburg, Austria
e-mail: christina.pichler@pmu.ac.at

© The Author(s) 2023
D. Spoladore et al. (eds.), *Digital and Strategic Innovation for Alpine Health Tourism*, SpringerBriefs in Applied Sciences and Technology, https://doi.org/10.1007/978-3-031-15457-7_1

Table 1 Alpine natural resources as basis for health tourism development

No.	Alpine natural health resource
1	Alpine farming & alpine pastures
2	Alpine hiking in high & moderate altitude
3	Alpine milk & dairy products
4	Balneotherapy/hydrotherapy/healing waters
5	Forest/forest therapy
6	Protected areas & biodiversity
7	Speleotherapy/radon therapy
8	Waterfalls
9	Winter activities

Nature-based Alpine health tourism can play a significant role in this context. The benefits of human interaction with natural Alpine health resources are manifold and range from acute stress relief [5], reduced symptoms of specific indications such as allergies and asthma and chronic low back pain [6–9] to improved immune responses [10], cardiorespiratory fitness and quality of life [11]. This exceptional healing potential builds a promising base for the development of evidence-based health tourism products and value chains that are mutually beneficial for tourists and local inhabitants in terms of sustainable regional development.

However, this potential has not yet been fully exploited by Alpine regions. There is obviously a lack of applicable knowledge on the health benefits of specific Alpine resources, resulting in an insufficient innovation capacity of tourism regions. Therefore, within the project HEALPS,[1] 20 Alpine health resources have been identified and characterized regarding their health tourism potential based on the available body of evidence. This research built the base for the project HEALPS2[2] that is focusing on the development of innovation strategies and hands-on tools to valorize this knowledge.

The present chapter highlights the results of the literature research on the health effects of Alpine health assets focusing on nine resources that are most promising for the development of evidence-based health tourism in terms of push & pull factors (see Table 1).

---

[1] *HEaling ALPS: Alpine Health Tourism: Positioning the Alpine region as globally attractive health promoting place.* The project was co-financed by the European Union (Alpine Region Preparatory Action Funds – ARPAF).

[2] *HEaling ALPS 2: Tourism based on natural health resources for the development of Alpine regions.* The project was co-financed by the European Union (European Regional Development Fund, Interreg Alpine Space 2014–2020) https://www.alpine-space.org/projects/healps-2.

2 Alpine Health Tourism Potential—Push And Pull Factors

The enormous health tourism potential of Alpine regions is not only made up of the unique health-promoting characteristics of Alpine natural resources—hereby referred to as *pull factors*—but also of the partly unhealthy habitats and resulting lifestyles in major source markets. The latter are referred to as *push factors* and are closely linked to the increasing global urbanization. The most relevant push factors in terms of health tourism are shortly described in the following.

2.1 Air Pollution

Environmental pollution is a major challenge to our modern society, as it is one of the most important threats to human health. Air pollution is composed of airborne particles and gaseous pollutants, such as nitrogen dioxide and ozone. Generally, airborne particles can be determined as ambient airborne particulate matter (PM), which is grouped as coarse, fine, and ultrafine particles (UFPs) with aerodynamic diameters within 2.5–10 μm (PM10), <2.5 μm (PM2.5) and <0.1 μm (PM0.1) [12].

A wide range of studies has documented the association of PM2.5 air pollution exposure with morbidity and mortality from respiratory and cardiovascular diseases. There is strong evidence that PM2.5 exposure attributes to specific diseases such as asthma, chronic obstructive pulmonary disease (COPD), pulmonary fibrosis, cancer, type-2 diabetes, neurodegenerative diseases, and even obesity [13–16].

From a geographic point of view, the Alpine region stands out in terms of air quality. Looking at an air quality map of Europe, the Alpine arc looks like a green island in a sea of grey fine dust, offering not only perfect conditions for diverse sports activities but also clean and fresh air [17].

2.2 Noise Pollution

An equally significant push factor is environmental noise exposure in relevant urban source markets. Environmental noise is defined as noise emitted from all sources except industrial workplaces. One in three individuals is annoyed during the daytime, and one in five has disturbed sleep at night because of traffic noise. There is sufficient evidence from large-scale epidemiological studies linking the populations' exposure to environmental noise with adverse health effects. Noise seriously harms human health and interferes with people's daily activities at school, at work, at home, and during leisure time. It can disturb sleep, cause cardiovascular and psychophysiological effects, reduce performance and provoke annoyance responses and changes in social behavior [18].

2.3 Reduced Microbial Diversity

Expanding urbanization is also a major factor behind rapidly declining biodiversity. Research suggests that in urbanized societies, the rarity of contact with diverse environmental microbiota negatively impacts immune function and ultimately increases the risk for allergies and other immune-mediated disorders [19].

Although further research is warranted, the microbial diversity of Alpine natural environments could be a promising development field for Alpine health tourism, e.g., regarding the prevention of allergies and asthma (see also Sects. 3.1 and 3.3).

2.4 Lack of Physical Exercise

Besides harmful environmental parameters, urbanization goes hand in hand with the development of sedentary lifestyles. The result of declining physical activity is an increase of disabilities and diseases [20, 21]. The pandemic of physical inactivity is associated with a range of chronic diseases and early deaths. Strong evidence shows that physical inactivity increases the risk of many adverse health conditions, such as the world's major non-communicable diseases (NCDs) of coronary heart disease, type 2 diabetes as well as breast and colon cancer. In addition, it is responsible for a substantial economic burden [22, 23].

Alpine regions offer a variety of sports opportunities, and holidays in Alpine regions are strongly associated with mountain hiking, biking, climbing, etc. Tailored health tourism products and services based on various physical exercise components could represent not only health benefits for tourists but also contribute to public health.

2.5 Loss of Contact with Nature

Another impact of increasing urbanization is the loss of contact with nature. This ongoing loss of human interaction with natural environments is viewed as one of the most fundamental obstacles to addressing global environmental challenges. Especially children are becoming less likely to have direct contact with nature. Research shows that children's affective attitudes and willingness to conserve biodiversity are positively associated with the frequency of both direct and vicarious experiences of nature. Children who frequently experience nature are likely to develop a greater emotional affinity to and support for protecting biodiversity. Therefore, children should be encouraged to experience nature and be provided with various types of nature experiences [24].

Moreover, being connected to nature and feeling happy are connected: People that are more connected to nature tend to experience more positive affect, vitality, and life satisfaction compared to those less connected to nature [25]. Nature-relatedness is furthermore a distinct predictor of many happiness indicators [26].

The desire to reconnect to nature offers a variety of opportunities for health tourism development in the Alpine region, especially in protected areas.

3 Evidence as a Strategic Development Factor in Alpine Health Tourism

Product authenticity in the sensitive field of personal health is an essential prerequisite for a responsible relationship with the guest. Therefore, the medical proof of expected respectively promised health effects is a condition 'sine qua non' in health tourism [27, 28] and referred to as *evidence-based*. This notion means that all health-related interventions within a tourism product must be developed and evaluated on the basis of the best available current scientific research and integrate guests' interests, values, and needs [29].

As research is growing in the field of nature-human interaction, evidence-based health tourism development is a promising strategy for innovative and sustainable regional development in the Alpine region. In the following, the health tourism potential of nine unique Alpine health resources is discussed, considering their respective body of evidence obtained from the biomedical database Pubmed [30]. The level of evidence regarding the individual publications refers to the system of six levels of evidence developed by the Agency for Healthcare Research and Quality [31] (see Table 2). Evidence level Ia represents the highest possible level of evidence, and evidence level IV the lowest. In this way, also research gaps were identified.

Table 2 Evidence levels of the agency for healthcare research and quality (AHRQ)

Level	Type of scientific evidence
Ia	Scientific evidence obtained from meta-analyses of randomized clinical trials
Ib	Scientific evidence obtained from at least one randomized clinical trial
IIa	Scientific evidence obtained from at least one well-designed, non-randomized prospective study
IIb	Scientific evidence obtained from at least one well-designed, quasi-experimental study
III	Scientific evidence obtained from well-designed observational studies, such as comparative studies, correlation study or case–control studies
IV	Scientific evidence obtained from documents or opinions of expert committees and/or clinical experience of renowned opinion leaders

3.1 Alpine Farming And Alpine Pastures

With regard to the health effects of Alpine farming and Alpine pastures, environmental microbes are of particular interest. The microbiome is currently a hot topic in the scientific community as well as in the mainstream media. Within the period of 2012–2017, the number of scientific publications increased by up to factor three [32]. Regarding asthma specifically, accumulating evidence indicates that the environmental microbiome plays a significant role in asthma development. The lower prevalence of asthma in populations exposed to farm environments indicates its potential for disease prevention. This protective effect is associated with the specific microbial diversity in a farming environment, especially those with livestock [33].

The human microbiome is defined as the collection of all microorganisms, including bacteria, archaea, and fungi, living in and on the bodies of humans. The microbiome seems to affect virtually every bodily function. Depending on its composition, it can produce thousands of different biologically active substances, including neurotransmitters such as dopamine, serotonin, and norepinephrine. According to the current state of science, the diversity of the microbiome seems to play the biggest role in human health. It is becoming increasingly apparent that the composition of the intestinal microbiome beginning in utero has long-term consequences on human health and well-being. It is therefore extremely important for the maintenance of health to allow the human microbiome to have a lively exchange with microbes from the environment. However, increasing urbanization and changing lifestyles (e.g., more sedentary lifestyles) reduce the spectrum of microorganisms we are exposed to. Studies show that people living in densely populated areas are less susceptible to microbial diversity than people living in rural neighborhoods, which also reduces the diversity of the human microbiome. There is emerging evidence that biodiversity loss in the wider environment might lead to reduced diversity in human microbiota, and these modifications are associated with a dramatic increase of immune-mediated diseases including metabolic, allergic, and inflammatory diseases and most likely also neurodegenerative and psychiatric disorders [32, 34–39].

Asthma and allergies are the most common chronic diseases in children and the leading causes of school absences, chronic medication usage, emergency department visits, and hospitalizations, which affect all members of the family and represent a significant societal and scientific challenge [40]. There is strong evidence that the development of allergic sensitization can be influenced by environmental co-factors. A large body of literature shows that children raised on farms have much lower rates of allergies and asthma. As early as the late 1990s, Von Ehrenstein and colleagues [41] as well as Riedler and colleagues [42, 43] found that farmer's children have a lower prevalence of hay fever, asthma, rhinoconjunctivitis as well as other atopic diseases and concluded that increased exposure to bacterial compounds in stables with livestock prevents the development of allergic disorders in children (level III). These findings could also be reproduced in other authors [see, e.g., 44–48]. There is a solid body of evidence that exposure to a greater variety of environmental microorganisms explains a substantial fraction of the inverse relation between asthma and growing up on a farm [49]. One key reason might be that the kids breathe in air full of molecules from the cell wall of certain bacteria, called lipopolysaccharides for their fat sugar structure. Also known as endotoxins, these fragments—from dying bacteria in cow manure and fodder—cause a temporary low state of inflammation in the lungs that somehow dampens the immune system's response to allergens [50]. Despite the protective effect of living on a farm, research suggests that even maternal exposure to an environment rich in microbial compounds might protect against the development of allergies and asthma and lead to an upregulation of receptors of the innate immune system [51].

Summarizing, the medical-scientific evidence shows great potential for the development of innovative health tourism products focusing on the prevention of allergies and asthma. Alpine farms and Alpine pastures could represent a valuable resource for city dwellers who are exposed to reduced microbial diversity in their everyday urban life. Current studies show that the timing of exposure to the farm environment is crucial: The strongest effects were observed for exposures that occurred in utero and during the first year of life [52]. Although, most studies in this field are retrospective cross-sectional studies (level III) and not experimental studies. This means that there is still a lack of evidence on the potential effect of health tourism stay on Alpine farms on the human microbiome. Considering the crucial timing of the exposure to farm environmental microbes, future research should focus on assessing the effect of holidays on Alpine farms and pastures for pregnant women or families with kids in their first year.

3.2 Alpine Hiking in High And Moderate Altitude

In the age of industrialization, holidays primarily focused on regeneration, rest, and recreation. The structural shift towards a service-oriented society has led to a change in holiday interests in the Western world. Although rest and recreation are still important to people during their holidays, the range of physical activities carried out while on holiday has grown considerably since the end of the 1990s. Especially hiking is becoming increasingly popular and represents an important travel motive [53]. The main reasons for hiking are experiencing nature, fresh air, the beauty of nature and landscape, fauna, and flora [54]. Another aspect that is becoming increasingly important is health as a motive for hiking holidays, and the scientific evidence of the positive effects of hiking on health and well-being is constantly growing. Exercise in natural environments reduces stress and protects against mental illness more effectively than does exercise in the city or indoors. From a physiological point of view, mountain hiking can be characterized as endurance exercise in nature with predominantly moderate intensity [55]. Thus, hiking is very well suited to respond to changing needs of vacation.

Therapies at moderate to high altitude (between 1500 and 3000 m above sea level) are known to affect a variety of physiological and immunological parameters. These include neurovegetative, cardiovascular, and thermoregulation mechanisms

[56, 57], but also the reduction of inflammation and immunomodulatory effects [58–60], while additional exercise in these altitudes leads to even stronger effects [61]. In contrast to UV radiation, which increases with rising sea level and is associated with vitamin D synthesis, fine dust pollution is reduced [17]. Furthermore, shorter flowering phases and more extreme weather conditions lead to a change in vegetation at higher altitudes, which significantly reduces allergen concentrations [62]. The lower air viscosity facilitates breathing and stays at moderate altitudes lead to relaxation and stress reduction [63]. Physical activity at moderate sea level leads to a significant increase in hematopoietic progenitor cells, promotes erythropoiesis, and thus increases the number of erythrocytes and oxygen supply [64]. Climate therapy at moderate to high altitude is also well-known as a successful alternative medical treatment for respiratory and allergic diseases such as bronchial asthma, atopic dermatitis, psoriasis or eczema [65–67].

One of the first approaches to investigate the health effects of Alpine mountain hiking were the "Austrian Moderate Altitude Studies" (AMAS) that were conducted in Austria. AMAS I (2000) focused on the indication of the metabolic syndrome, a combination of overweight, disturbed blood sugar and blood fat metabolism as well as elevated blood pressure, which are massive cardiovascular risk factors, whereas AMAS II (2006) focused on persons with high-stress levels. The studies proved that an active sojourn (a combination of hiking and active/passive regeneration) at Alpine moderate altitudes (1500–2500 m) under the guidance of professional coaches has positive effects in probands with metabolic syndrome as well as in a clientele suffering from stress [68–70]. In addition, physical activity in nature is subjectively perceived as less strenuous, while mental exhaustion and stress levels are reduced. Physical activity in nature also has a mood-lifting effect, increases self-confidence, and the personal state of health is subjectively rated higher. In addition, attention and the ability to concentrate are increased [10, 71–74].

Niedermeier et al. [74] were able to show in a randomized crossover study that the stress hormone cortisol can be reduced by three hours of mountain hiking with 600 m altitude difference to a greater extent than by relaxation in a quiet place. Walking is good for the bones, prevents osteoporosis-related complaints, and also sustainably increases health-related quality of life (HRQOL), and reduces pain in the 50–65 age group studied [75]. Three-week mountain hiking improves blood pressure and pulse behavior so effectively that even antihypertensive drugs could be reduced and partially discontinued. The body weight decreased significantly, and the vitalizing red blood corpuscles increased. In addition, quality of life improved, and quality of sleep was also positively influenced [68, 76, 77].

Mountain hiking combines concentric and eccentric training: When walking uphill, the muscle overcomes gravity by contracting or shortening the muscle fibers (= concentric). The main load factor in uphill walking is, therefore, almost exclusively concentric. Walking downhill, on the other hand, requires the muscle to counteract gravity by lengthening in a controlled manner (= eccentric). Regular eccentric training leads to positive adaptations in the areas of strength and kinematics (biomechanics). In addition, positive metabolic adaptations can be induced by eccentric loads. Due to the lower cardiopulmonary load, people with cardiovascular diseases (e.g., in the initial rehabilitation phase) can also benefit from this form of exercise. For people with low cardiorespiratory fitness, walking downhill is ideal training for later tours with a slight ascent [78].

During mountain hiking, mountaineers are confronted with often rapidly changing environmental conditions like slope of the path, stony or narrower passages, altitude, weather conditions, ascending and descanting sections. These constantly changing conditions require constant proprioceptive feedback, thus promoting the diversification of gait patterns and balance responses [79]. Mountain hiking could therefore be an effective training for older people, addressing both aerobic capacity, strength, and balance.

The health tourism potential of Alpine hiking can be seen as very high in Alpine regions. In product development, it should ideally be combined with other location-bound natural resources that could provide additional health benefits, such as balneotherapy or waterfalls. The beneficial effects of balneotherapy are widely used to treat musculoskeletal diseases, to improve immunity, and relieve pain [80]. Bathing in thermal water triggers several physiological responses like vasodilation, gate control mechanism, elevation of beta-endorphin levels, and muscle relaxation, which could positively affect regeneration after exercise like, e.g., mountain hiking. The additional integration of location-bound resources contributes to the development of a unique health tourism appeal as they are geographically specific and cannot be exported [29]. Another element for health tourism differentiation in the field of mountain hiking is the development of target group-specific products. Hiking trails have different characteristics that can be developed for specific indications like, e.g., cardiorespiratory fitness, chronic low back pain, etc.

3.3 Alpine Milk And Dairy Products

An old farmer's proverb says that the grass is always better the higher one goes, and at the top it is so good that even farmers might like to eat it. In fact, with increasing elevation, plant growth diminishes and with it the yields; but since the intensity of sunshine increases, Alpine plants process greater amounts of energy that leads to a higher protein and fat content. Animals react in a similar manner. Because of the demands of Alpine living on their bodies, animals are slower to fatten than during the same length of time in the valley, and milk output at higher altitudes is much lower than in the valleys. Although, it is also creamier when manufactured at higher elevations. Still today, it contains between 15 and 30% more fat than in the valley. What is more, Alpine products were considered to be tastier and healthier because of herbs found only there, containing high percentages of ethereal oils [81].

The local flavor of the high mountainous meadows shows up in their products, which is why the cheeses were named after the Alpine pastures where they were produced. Urnerbödeler, Saanen, or Emmentaler cheese: whole regions were identified with certain types of cheese. The links between landscape, animal, and product represented a strain of thought with several components. The notion of dairy practices encompassed perceptions about the influence of the terrain on plants, animals, and their products. When the first naturalists and doctors directed their attention to the Alps, they soon discovered these links. Hippolyt Guarinoni, a doctor and humanist in the sixteenth century, stated, e.g. that the products of the lowlands could not match the quality of Alpine products [81].

Dairy production therefore has a long tradition in the Alpine region and has soon been associated with beneficial health outcomes. Milk and its derivates are useful foods throughout all life periods, in particular during childhood and adolescence, as their contents of calcium, protein, phosphorus, and other micronutrients can promote skeletal, muscular, and neurologic development. Especially Alpine milk and Alpine dairy products seem to have a health-promoting nutritional value due to their composition. Generally, milk from grass-fed livestock is more beneficial than that of corn-fed animals [82]. It could be shown that cheese made from cows grazed on Alpine pastures have a more favorable fatty acid profile than other cheese types. Alpine cheese may be a relevant source of Alpha-Linolenic acid (ALA), which is cardioprotective [83].

Several studies also show that—especially unpasteurized—Alpine milk consumption may prevent the development of allergies and asthma. Similar to the exposure to environmental microbes on farms, farm milk consumption during pregnancy and early childhood shows the strongest effect. However, it has to be mentioned that most studies are cross-sectional (level IIa) [84, 85]. These associations do not confirm a causal relationship, and further investigation to identify specific protective agents or mechanisms is required. Some cohort studies have already been undertaken that support the protective effect of milk consumption (level III) [42, 86]. Although, more cohort studies are necessary to clarify the temporal sequence of exposure and outcome to identify critical periods of childhood when exposure to these putative protective agents or mechanisms might operate. It is also important to mention that unpasteurized milk consumption is not hazard-free, as milk-related outbreaks of Cryptosporidium species, Campylobacter species, and Escherichia coli O157 have been described [87]. Therefore, it is important to understand which components and mechanisms are underlying the observed protective effects and risks to ultimately be able to utilize milk as a means of primary prevention. Until then, the consumption of raw milk cannot be safely recommended [88].

Nevertheless, Alpine dairy production plays a key role in the protection of the Alpine flora and fauna as well as in the preservation of regionally typical landscapes. It is also integral to the ecological structure and cultural identity [81] and can therefore be a valuable product component in Alpine health tourism.

3.4 Balneotherapy/Hydrotherapy/Healing Waters

Balneotherapy has a long tradition in Alpine regions and is traditionally used for a variety of medical indications like rheumatic, dermatological, pulmonary, or gynecological problems, but especially for disease prevention, stress reduction, and recreation [89]. The terms balneotherapy, hydrotherapy, and spa therapy are often used interchangeably, which is also due to different meanings in different regions and cultures. Generally, balneotherapy involves immersion in mineral and/or thermal waters from natural springs, while hydrotherapy employs normal tap water for medical treatment. Balneotherapy is traditionally practiced in health resorts respectively spa towns with their special therapeutic atmosphere as part of a complex therapy program, which is why the term balneotherapy is often used synonymously for spa therapy. Although, strictly speaking, spa therapy employs a number of different treatment modalities, including hydro- and balneotherapy that is often combined with massage, exercise, physical therapy and/or rehabilitation. Obviously, this lack of consensus on terminology as well as the regional and cultural differences regarding the application of balneotherapy, represent a major barrier in medical research and reduce the performance of meta-analyses and systematic reviews [90]. This has to be taken into account when assessing the medical evidence of Alpine balneotherapeutic interventions. Considering the sheer amount of studies on balneotherapy, the focus here is on the highest evidence level, namely systematic reviews.

To date, there are three Cochrane[3] reviews (level Ia) on balneotherapy focusing on indications that are commonly treated with balneotherapy: osteoarthritis, rheumatoid arthritis, and venous insufficiency. Regarding osteoarthritis, it was found that spending time in a mineral bath compared to no treatment may improve pain and quality of life [92]. Pain severity of patients with rheumatoid arthritis can also be reduced through balneotherapy. Although, the overall evidence is insufficient to show that balneotherapy is more effective than no treatment due to the low quality of the provided studies that could be included in the review [93]. Finally, the review on chronic venous insufficiency provides evidence of low to moderate certainty in the choice of balneotherapy in quality of life, pain, and changes in skin pigmentation. Most individual studies report positive results but do not provide sufficient evidence to support the data due to the small number of participants and limited data [94].

In summarizing, the strength of the body of evidence regarding balneotherapy is insufficient and positive outcomes of individual studies should be viewed with caution. This is not due to the general lack of medical research in this field but due to the poor methodological quality of studies. There is a high risk of bias in most studies as well as a lack of adequate statistical analysis and data presentation [92, 94].

Balneo- respectively spa therapy is a huge economic factor for many Alpine regions. Although, public cutbacks have put increasing strain on many balneary regions and spa towns. Health insurances incrementally ask for reliable evidence on the effects of the individual therapy. Therefore, high-quality research is needed,

---

[3] The Cochrane Database of Systematic Reviews (CDSR) is the leading journal and database for systematic reviews in health care [91]

focusing on appropriate allocation concealment as well as adequate data analysis and presentation [92, 94]. Furthermore, future studies should also conduct cost-effectiveness analyses, as these could be a valuable argument when it comes to resource allocation in healthcare policy [90].

One approach to innovative research in health tourism regarding balneotherapy is to assess not only the effect of the individual balneotherapeutic therapy but to assess the potential benefits of a whole health tourism product in comparison to a standard holiday. Using this approach, Prossegger and colleagues [80] could show that a seven-day intervention with moderate mountain hiking in combination with balneotherapy is an effective training for older persons, inducing short-term improvements in static balance and quality of life. Based on these findings, regional health tourism development processes were initiated, and target group-specific products and service chains were created and positioned on the market [95].

3.5 Forest/Forest Therapy

In recent years, there has been considerable and increasing attention to using the forest environment as a place for recreation and health promotion. This trend derives from Japan, where it is called "shinrin-yoku", which is a term that means "taking in the forest atmosphere through all of our senses" or simpler "forest bathing". Since the development of the concept during the 1980s, considerable scientific research on its health effects and the mechanisms behind the healing effects was conducted [96]. The first studies were conducted on the Japanese island Yakushima (shima = island in Japanese). Yakushima includes a $\approx$19,000 ha area as a biosphere reserve. The island is located at a biogeographic boundary between tropical and temperate regions and contains a remarkably wide variety of flora: There are evergreen broadleaf forests, conifer, 2000-year-old cedar trees, and nearly 2000 different plant species [73]. Most other forest study sites have similar characteristics. This is important to mention when it comes to discussing the transferability of study results from tropical/south Asian forests to European resp. Alpine forests. Reported health benefits from forest therapy studies include impacts on humans' immune system, boosting natural killer cells and anticancer proteins, reduced stress, improved mood, sleep, and well-being, reduced blood pressure, accelerated recovery from illness, and increased ability to concentrate [97–100]. Based on these results, more than 50 Forest Therapy Trails were developed in Japan with millions of annual visitors, and forest therapy has become a cornerstone of preventive health care and healing in Japanese medicine. Also, in other Asian countries like China and South Korea, forest therapy has become very popular, and the trend is now also emerging in Europe [101].

There are more than 150 publications on forest therapy (including keywords "shinrin-yoku", "forest therapy", and "forest bath") listed in PubMed [30]. Despite this large body of literature, the evidence base for health benefits attributable to forest therapy is rather low due to methodological weaknesses. Oh and colleagues [102] conducted a systematic review on forest therapy, where only six randomized controlled trials (RCT, highest evidence regarding single intervention studies) met the inclusion criteria. These criteria were based on the assessment of methodological quality according to the Cochrane risk of bias (ROB) tool. The review found that the included six RCTs reported promising therapeutic benefits of forest exposure on several physical and psychological conditions, including hypertension, cardiac and pulmonary function, stress, immune function, inflammation, oxidative stress, stress hormones, anxiety and depression, and emotional response; although, outcomes of anxiety and depression had mixed results and some inflammatory biomarkers showed no results. The review concludes that there is a consistent trend in a broad range of health outcomes, suggesting potential for forest bathing. Although, the authors state that the included studies had a high risk of bias. Due to this lack of high-quality studies, there is no convincing evidence of the benefits of forest therapy. Furthermore, none of these studies were registered in the international trial registry.

Within five years since the publication of Oh and colleagues' review, only six further randomized controlled trials were published (also not registered at the ISRCTN). Two of them were conducted in China and showed beneficial effects on patients with chronic heart failure [103, 104] (level Ib). Another study from China examined the psychological effects of forest therapy [105]. Also, in China, Kim and Shin [106] investigated whether there is a difference between guided and self-guided forest therapy (level IIa). In both cases, positive psychological effects have been shown, but they do not seem to be generally transferable. The remaining two studies were conducted in Denmark and Sweden and could not show any difference between forest therapy and control group regarding physiological parameters [107, 108] (level Ib and IIa). However, both studies found positive effects on psychological parameters such as stress and anxiety. A recent pilot study from Italy also focuses on psychological effects and confirmed the positive effects on stress and anxiety [109] (level IIa).

Besides the lack of methodological quality, there are further limitations on the transferability of study results to Alpine forests. Research suggests that many measured health effects are attributed to phytoncides, which is a generalized term for natural chemicals released by plants into the environment. It is theorized that these chemicals could influence stress physiology and immunology through inhalation. Most forest therapy studies were conducted in tropical primeval forests (mostly Japanese, Korean, and Chinese) with a high biodiversity [73]. These forests are totally different from typical Alpine forests. Almost all Alpine forests are semi-natural, as defined by Forest Europe, with a significant presence of large trees and deadwood. There are almost no truly primary forests and plantations [110]. Thus, also their phytoncide composition is totally different. The measured effects can therefore not be transferred to Alpine forests. In most studies, the control group stayed in Asian megacities like Tokyo, with high air and noise pollution. The measured health benefits can, therefore, also be attributed to the absence of these factors. Furthermore, these cities are not comparable to typical European/Alpine cities. Additionally, most studies on forest therapy have been conducted with male Asian subjects [111], which is a further limitation on transferability. An approach to analyzing the health potential of alpine forests according to current medical scientific standards is shown by

Pichler and colleagues in their method paper presenting a randomized controlled clinical trial that compares two types of nature-based interventions in South Tyrol [112].

Considering the rich occurrence of forests in the Alpine region and the emerging trend towards nature-based recreation, forests may be considered as an important resource with a high health tourism potential. As a base for health-promoting activities, forests not only offer potential for longer stays: also, short-term stays seem to have a positive effect, especially on psychological aspects of stress and anxiety. In this respect, forests can also be thought in terms of a local health-promoting recreation for urban areas. However, based on current data, no scientifically founded statement can be made about the specific health effects of Alpine forests.

3.6 Protected Areas And Biodiversity

The Alps are among the richest regions of Europe regarding the variety of landscapes as well as plant and animal species. As the loss or destruction of habitats is the most direct threat to biodiversity, protected areas are crucial to counter the continuing loss of ecosystems and species [113]. There are nearly 1000 protected areas in the Alps, covering a surface area of over 53,000 km^2. The protected areas cover roughly 28% of the Alps [114]. The Alps are thereby one of the world's most important ecoregions in terms of conserving global biodiversity [113].

According to the Convention on Biological Diversity (Article 2), biodiversity means the variability among living organisms from all sources, including inter alia, terrestrial, marine, and other aquatic ecosystems and the ecological complexes of which they are part. This variability includes diversity within species, between species, and of ecosystems. This definition reflects different levels of biodiversity, including genetic diversity, species, and ecosystems [115].

Closely linked to biodiversity is the environmental microbial diversity that influences the human microbiome, which is the collection of microorganisms including bacteria, archaea, and fungi living in and on the bodies of humans. This is an emerging research field in medical science and holds significant health tourism potential as a specific Alpine resource.

Biodiversity and human health are interlinked in various ways. A large body of papers regarding the effects of protected areas on human health focuses on the provision of ecosystem services. For example, Harrison et al. [116] showed that nearly two-thirds of the global population rely directly on protected areas for freshwater provision. Also, protected areas play an important role in providing pollination services for food production or in contributing to air purification and temperature regulation. Another important role of protected areas is the conservation of medical plants and the numerous recreational services provided by protected areas that promote a healthy lifestyle [117]. The most well-researched aspect of the direct link between protected areas and human health is the effect on psychosocial well-being. Protective areas have a strong restorative capacity and have shown to foster recovery from mental fatigue, reduce stress levels, assist cognitive functioning, and improve the overall psychological state [117, 118]. Some studies show that these psychological benefits are higher in areas of greater biodiversity [119, 120]. Furthermore, research indicates a potential beneficial and protective influence of residential areas with a high biodiversity on respiratory health [121].

Studies that contribute to the understanding of positive health outcomes of protected areas and biodiversity are mostly conducted in Australia [120, 121] or Scandinavia [122]. No intervention study could be identified that explicitly links Alpine-specific protected areas to direct health outcomes.

Although, based on the indirect links of protected areas and biodiversity to human health and well-being, it is evident from the authors' perspective that there is a huge health tourism potential. Also, protected areas play a key role in the conservation of other Alpine natural resources with medical-scientific proof, such as waterfalls, and can therefore be seen as "meta health resources". However, the research base regarding studies that specifically address the role of protected areas in supporting human health is generally low. Biodiversity-health linkages have often been explored by looking at ecosystem service flows like, for example, water and energy provision but are rarely taking protected areas as a leading analytical unit. Consequently, health outcomes of protected areas have been largely overlooked [117]. Therefore, there is both a strong need and potential for research programs that foster health-biodiversity linkages, especially in terms of Alpine protected areas. To fully exploit the resulting health tourism potential, research projects should be characterized by a strong integration of the protected area's management and the tourism industry.

3.7 Speleotherapy/Radon Therapy

Speleotherapy is a special kind of climate therapy which uses the specific microclimate of mines and caves to treat especially respiratory and skin-related diseases. Speleotherapy is relatively widespread in Europe. Speleotherapy facilities vary in their environmental conditions, including radiation level, temperature, and humidity. In most caves, patients are advised to rest during this period. In some caves, physical exercises or breathing exercises, including the inhalation of salt aerosols, are recommended.

A meta-analysis of the health effect of Speleotherapy with respect to chronic asthma was conducted by Beamon et al. [123] (level Ia). Only three studies met the inclusion criteria. This already shows the problem that there are too few studies to date to be able to make a reliable statement on the effect of Speleotherapy. Therefore, the authors conclude that further randomized controlled trials with long-term follow-ups are necessary. Gaus and Weber [124] demonstrated that a 3-week Speleotherapy intervention significantly improved the FEV-1[4] of children aged 4–10 years with bronchial asthma up to one week after intervention. Although, it is not clear from this study whether a long-term improvement can be induced. However, it was shown that Speleotherapy is an efficient and safe form of therapy for children with bronchial asthma. Overall, there is little scientific evidence on Speleotherapy. Caves and mines differ in their specific conditions. Therefore, further research is needed to evaluate its specific effects.

One form of Speleotherapy is based on the use of radon. Since the beginning of the twentieth century, radon therapy has been applied in middle Europe. Radon therapy uses the chemically inert naturally radioactive gas radon to treat various diseases. Its main application is found as a non-pharmacological treatment option for various inflammatory rheumatic diseases. For treatment purposes, radon is commonly applied by bathing for about 20 min in water with a radon concentration of 0.3–3 kBq/L or staying for about 1 h in caves or galleries with natural radon concentrations of about 30–160 kBq/m3.

Currently, relevant studies on radon are available for different indications. A meta-analysis of Falkenbach et al. [125] examines the effect of radon therapy, including Radon Balneotherapy and Speleotherapy, on pain reduction in rheumatic diseases (degenerative spinal disease, rheumatoid arthritis, and ankylosing spondylitis) (level Ia). No immediate effects were found, but significant improvements in pain were found three and six months after treatment. Overall, however, the meta-analysis concludes that further studies on radon therapy are needed. Other studies are concerned with the treatment of rheumatoid arthritis and osteoporosis. Osteoporosis is a widespread systemic skeletal disease characterized by decreased bone mass. Secondary osteoporosis is a frequent complication of rheumatoid arthritis. Winkelmayr et al. [75] compared low-dose radon hyperthermia treatment with either radon thermal water or radon-free thermal water in combination with mountain hiking (level Ib). Both interventions produced statistically equal results: Significant immediate and long-term effects on regulators of bone metabolism and somatic complaints were observed. Another study of low-dose radon hyperthermia therapy examined the effects of hyperthermia treatment on osteoporosis in patients with rheumatoid arthritis compared with patients with osteoarthritis [126]. Serial low-dose radon hyperthermia therapy causes an increase in bone-building cytokines and a decrease in bone-catabolic cytokines in rheumatoid arthritis. Also dealing with rheumatoid arthritis were Franke et al. [127] (level Ib). This study investigated the effects of radon baths on rheumatoid arthritis in contrast to artificial CO_2 baths. Long-term improvements in pain intensity, as well as reduced doses of corticosteroids and NSAIDs (non-steroidal anti-inflammatory drugs) and/or analgesics, were observed in the radon group. On the same topic, a multi-center study investigated the effects of radon spa therapy in comparison to placebo applied on health resort out-patients [128]. Radon spa therapy improved pain relief and analgesic drug consumption. No

---

[4] The forced expiratory volume in 1 s (FEV1) is the volume of air (in liters) exhaled in the first second during forced exhalation after maximal inspiration and is an important diagnostic parameter in lung diseases.

effects regarding quality of life were observed. Significant benefits were found until six months follow-up, but not until nine months follow-up. In a pilot study, beneficial effects of radon spa therapy on the total antioxidant status were observed [129]. In addition, Passali et al. [130] analyzed the effect of radon hot spring therapy in a narrative review that included four prospective studies. Considered were asthma, respiratory tract inflammation, and nasal obstruction, and allergic rhinitis. Improvements in nasal resistance, air flow, mucociliary clearance, and ciliated to muciparous cell ratio and FEV-1 in asthmatic patients were observed. Finally, a study on pain and hypertension investigated the effect of low-dose radon spa therapy [131]. Patients with chronic painful musculoskeletal diseases received either radon balneotherapy or radon CO_2 balneotherapy. The radon CO_2 treatment effectively relieved pain. Furthermore, a reduction in blood pressure could be observed in patients who received the radon CO_2 treatment.

Apart from the therapeutic application of Speleotherapy, the historical caves and tunnels are very well suited for the creation of unique experiences and educational purposes. In this way, they have the capacity to meet leisure, tourism, and healthcare needs.

3.8 Waterfalls

The Alpine region hosts numerous waterfalls that produce nano-aerosol, a particularly valuable feature in terms of the healing potential of the Alpine region. Nano-aerosols are nanometer-sized electrically charged atomized water droplets of waterfalls. The charged nano-aerosol is formed within microseconds after the ionization of primary ions due to hydration and cluster ion formation processes. Waterfalls mainly produce negatively charged ions, referred to as 'Lenard ions'. As a result of the aerosolized water hitting the ground, the droplets created in the waterfall form dipoles with a negatively charged surface. Due to the waterfall wind, the negatively charged particles, atomized by thermophoretic processes, drift away from the waterfall, whereas the positively charged droplets quickly sink to the ground. This causes a surplus of negatively charged air ions in the proximity of the waterfalls, which can be of the order of several 10.000 ions/cm3 of air. The diameter of these negative air ions is between 1.5 and 10 nm, whereby 2 nm sized negative ions are most abundant. Their lifetime is long enough to be inhaled. The remaining bigger fragments are positive and precipitate to the ground [132–134].

Traditionally, numerous beneficial health effects have been attributed to waterfalls. Although, to date, only a few waterfalls have been evaluated according to the criteria of evidence-based medicine regarding their potential health benefits. The first randomized clinical trial (RCT, level Ib) on this was conducted by the research group of Arnulf Hartl at the Paracelsus Medical University in Salzburg, who assessed the Krimml waterfall aerosol's effect on clinical, functional, molecular and immunological parameters of allergic asthma. Imbedded in an asthma camp, 54 children aged 8–14 with mild to moderate bronchial asthma spent three weeks in the National Park

Hohe Tauern in the Federal State of Salzburg, Austria. The patients were divided into two groups: Both groups spent a daily hour outdoor exposition, the waterfall group close to the Krimml waterfalls and the control group 6 km away. Living, housing and nutrition, and other daily activities were completely identical in both groups. Over the three weeks of exposure, the waterfall caused a balancing immune modulation characterized by a change in the ratio of allergic/anti-allergic regulatory T-cells. While both groups benefited from the high-altitude therapy in the National Park Hohe Tauern in terms of a reduction of asthmatic symptoms, only exposure to the waterfall improved pulmonary function by 30% with a measurable effective duration of at least two months. Furthermore, the asthmatic symptoms of the waterfall group were significantly alleviated compared to the control group even four months after exposure [134, 135].

Also, the second RCT (level Ib) on the effect of waterfall aerosols was conducted in the National Park Hohe Tauern, although in their southern Carinthian part at the Gartl waterfall. In a three-armed RCT, the effect of the waterfall was assessed on immunological reagibility, physiological stress, and stress-related psychological parameters. People with moderate to high stress level spent an active sojourn with daily hiking tours in the National Park Hohe Tauern, Carinthia, Austria. Additionally to hiking, half of the group was exposed to the Gartl waterfall aerosol for one hour a day, while the other half of the group spent the same time at a distant site at the same altitude. A third control group stayed at home. Results showed an improvement of lung function and most physiological stress parameters in both intervention groups compared to the control group. Additionally, waterfall-specific positive effects on the immunological reagibility as well as on psychological stress parameters were found. Thus, the study data indicate an influence of the waterfall ionosols on complex psychoneuroimmunological regulatory circuits [10], which could be the basis for the development of health tourism products and service chains focusing on the prevention and therapy of chronic stress.

The health tourism potential of Alpine waterfalls is enormous. For example, based on the medical research of the Krimml waterfalls, the health tourism initiative 'Hohe Tauern Health' was developed that promotes evidence-based health tourism products for the target group of allergic and asthmatic guests [136]. This initiative has developed into a major economic and innovation factor as it led to the creation and higher qualification of job profiles and triggered cross-sectorial regional innovations such as allergy-friendly timber construction [137].

Although every waterfall has its own physical signature and different waterfalls thus have different effects on human physiology [138]. Therefore, the development of health tourism products based on the health effects of Alpine waterfalls has to go hand in hand with medical research, ideally with a clinical study on the potential health benefit of the individual waterfall.

3.9 Winter Activities

During winter, cities in major Alpine source markets are often characterized by a high level of air pollution. In addition to the year-round fine dust producers such as traffic etc., the heating period significantly increases particulate matter emissions. Furthermore, temperature inversion leads to increased winter smog. Compared to urban environments, fine dust pollution is extremely low in Alpine mountainous regions, and they are therefore perfectly suited for exercise in clean and fresh air.

Winter activities in Alpine regions are still predominantly snow-based, like Alpine skiing, cross-country skiing, ski mountaineering, and snowshoeing. Alpine skiing is the main reason for winter holidays in the Alps. Besides its fun factor, it also has positive effects on our health and well-being. It is e.g. an efficient way to increase cardiorespiratory fitness, measured in increased maximum oxygen uptake (VO2max) [139] (level IIb). Skiing primarily trains leg muscles, but arm and upper body muscles are also exerted. Considering the breaks during lift rides, Alpine skiing burns about 400 kcal per hour. However, the study by Stöggl et al. only considered high-intensity Alpine ski training. Since skiing promotes leg strength and balance, it can be an effective preventive measure for the growing target group of best agers (60 years and older) to maintain physical fitness and prevent falls. These positive effects were confirmed by Muller et al. [140] in a study with an investigation period of twelve weeks (level Ib). Skiing also reduces cardiovascular risk factors and prevents atherosclerosis and type 2 diabetes, and is also a safe exercise for elderly people regarding cardiovascular risks [141–143] (all level Ib). A reduced sympathetic activity induced by skiing was found in middle-aged men, which has an additional cardioprotective effect [144] (level Iib).

Cross-country skiing is another winter sport that offers a wide range of health benefits, while there is only a low risk of injury and sports-related consequential damages:

Cross country skiing is a full-body workout that uses and strengthens all major muscle groups in arms, chest, back, abdominals and legs. Furthermore, cross-country skiing is an excellent training for the improvement of cardiorespiratory fitness: cross-country skiers exhibit some of the highest maximal oxygen uptake (VO2max) values [145] (level Iib). Within one hour, about 800–1000 kcal are burned during cross-country skiing. Research shows that cross-country skiers suffer less frequently from overweight, show better health behavior, and their risk of developing cardiovascular disease is significantly decreased [146] (level III). Furthermore, the risk of cancer, as well as the overall mortality rate, is reduced, as shown in a cohort study comparing Swedish cross-country skiers with the general population [147]. A follow-up Finnish population study with over 2000 participants confirmed these results by showing that general mortality is inversely and independently associated with frequency and duration of recreational cross-country skiing [148] (level III).

Ski mountaineering is one of the leading trends in Alpine winter sports. The rewarding effect of an adventurous descent on ungroomed slopes after a strenuous climb through untouched winter landscapes clearly has addictive potential. However, in order to prevent injuries a certain level of fitness is required. Ski mountaineering is a high-intensity sport and is, therefore, an excellent training for the improvement of cardiorespiratory fitness [149] (level III). Consequently, the prevalence of cardiovascular diseases in ski mountaineers is much lower compared to the general population [150] (level III). Furthermore, ski mountaineering does not only train endurance and strength, but can also be used as a recovery and regeneration measure [151]. Haslinger and colleagues could show that ski mountaineering is even safe for people with total knee arthroplasty [152].

Snowshoeing is an Alpine winter sport that can be compared to Nordic Walking. It is a full-body exercise that is easy on the joints and suitable for all ages and fitness levels. Snowshoeing burns up to twice the number of calories as walking at the same speed (up to 1.000 cal per hour) [153]. Furthermore, in comparison to walking, snowshoeing recruits more muscle groups. Especially for women, often wearing high-heels snowshoeing can be beneficial, as negative effects like a tightening of the hamstring can be counteracted [154].

Considering the need for winter product differentiation with regard to climate change as well as changing customer demands, winter hiking is a promising field of development. It is possible on all hiking trails that are approved and mapped as such in terms of avalanche danger and walkability in winter. The calorie consumption for one hour of winter hiking is around 250 kcal. Exercise in fresh air and sun releases the happiness hormone serotonin, which counteracts both physical stress reactions and the "winter blues" thus lifting mood [155, 156]. Winter hiking also reduces physiological parameters such as blood pressure and heart rate, supports weight loss and improves cholesterol and sugar metabolism [70, 76, 157, 158]. It is particularly suitable for overweight people and those affected by metabolic syndrome (high blood pressure, abdominal obesity, fat metabolism disorders, and increased blood sugar). Furthermore, winter hiking in moderately cold temperatures reduces airway inflammation levels (measured as fractional concentration of exhaled nitric oxide (FeNo)) as well as the number of eosinophil cells in the nose and induces sustainable improvements of allergic symptoms [80] (level Ib). Winter hiking is suitable for all age groups and can especially address families.

Currently, health tourism offers and initiatives predominantly focus on summer holidays, whereas the health tourism potentials in Alpine winter tourism have not yet been exploited. As shown above, also the winter season offers a variety of opportunities to develop evidence-based health tourism products. Furthermore, the development of winter health tourism products can be a strategy to react to the already noticeable impacts of climate change with rising snowlines and shorter winter seasons. Especially winter hiking products can contribute to a diversified product range to reduce snow-reliance.

4 Conclusion

Evidence-based health effects of Alpine natural resources are a promising starting point for the development of health tourism products and enhance the innovation capacity of tourism regions. The presented body of evidence regarding the health benefits of nine selected Alpine resources highlights the enormous health tourism potential but also reveals research gaps. Moreover, it was demonstrated that not every measured health benefit of a specific and location-bound health resource is transferable to the same resource in another region: The example of Alpine waterfalls shows that similar resources may trigger different health effects. Therefore, when regional health tourism development processes are initiated, there is a strong need for early integration of medical research and intense dialogue between tourism and medicine throughout the development process. Furthermore, a successful health tourism product is in most cases, not solely based on one specific resource but combines the unique assets of the individual region—not only in terms of natural environments but also in terms of culture, services, cuisine or infrastructure. An approach to the assessment and evidence-based combination of these regional key performance indicators (KPIs) is presented in the contribution in this book by Bischof & Hartl "KPI for data-driven assessment and benchmarking of potential development paths for nature-based health tourism in the Alpine region".

As Alpine tourism regions are required to differentiate their tourism products to compete in an increasingly competitive and cluttered global market, the valorization of Alpine natural health resources and other unique regional assets represents a crucial success factor for tourism innovation and regional development strategies. If the resulting regional development processes follow a science- and sustainability-driven approach, each resulting health tourism product will contribute to the positioning of the Alpine region as a globally attractive health-promoting place for guests and the local inhabitants, while promoting local competence and future-proof value creation.

References

1. P.L. Winter, S. Selin, L. Cerveny, K. Bricker, Outdoor recreation, nature-based tourism, and sustainability. Sustainability **12**, 81 (2019). https://doi.org/10.3390/su12010081
2. H. Frumkin, N.G. Bratman, J.S. Breslow, B. Cochran, K.P.H. Jr, J.J. Lawler, S.P. Levin, S.P. Tandon, U. Varanasi, L.K. Wolf, A.S. Wood, Nature contact and human health: a research agenda. Environ. Health Perspect. **125** (2017). https://doi.org/10.1289/EHP1663
3. T. Hartig, R. Mitchell, S. de Vries, H. Frumkin, Nature and health. Annu. Rev. Public Health. **35**, 207–28 (2014). 10/f2qr98. https://doi.org/10.1146/annurev-publhealth-032013-182443
4. J.M. Robinson, P. Brindley, R. Cameron, D. MacCarthy, A. Jorgensen, Nature's role in supporting health during the COVID-19 pandemic: a geospatial and socioecological study. Int. J. Environ. Res. Public Health. **18**, 2227 (2021). https://doi.org/10.3390/ijerph18052227
5. M. Niedermeier, C. Grafetstätter, A. Hartl, M. Kopp, A randomized crossover trial on acute stress-related physiological responses to mountain Hiking. Int. J. Environ. Res. Public Health. **14** (2017). https://doi.org/10/gbv8kt

6. M. Gaisberger, R. Šanović, H. Dobias, P. Kolarž, A. Moder, J. Thalhamer, A. Selimović, I. Huttegger, M. Ritter, A. Hartl, Effects of ionized waterfall aerosol on pediatric allergic asthma. J. Asthma. **49**, 830–838 (2012). https://doi.org/10/gc3khp
7. J. Freidl, D. Huber, H. Braunschmid, C. Romodow, C. Pichler, R. Weisböck-Erdheim, M. Mayr, A. Hartl, Winter exercise and speleotherapy for allergy and asthma: a randomized controlled clinical trial. J. Clin. Med. **9** (2020). https://doi.org/10/ghg8hq
8. J. Prossegger, D. Huber, C. Grafetstätter, C. Pichler, H. Braunschmid, R. Weisböck-Erdheim, A. Hartl, Winter exercise reduces allergic airway inflammation: a randomized controlled study. Int. J. Environ. Res. Public Health. **16** (2019). https://doi.org/10/gf32db
9. D. Huber, C. Grafetstätter, J. Proßegger, C. Pichler, E. Wöll, M. Fischer, M. Dürl, K. Geiersperger, M. Höcketstaller, S. Frischhut, M. Ritter, A. Hartl, Green exercise and mg-ca-SO4 thermal balneotherapy for the treatment of non-specific chronic low back pain: a randomized controlled clinical trial. BMC Musculoskelet Disord. **20**, 221 (2019). https://doi.org/10/gf3k72
10. C. Grafetstätter, M. Gaisberger, J. Prossegger, M. Ritter, P. Kolarž, C. Pichler, J. Thalhamer, A. Hartl, Does waterfall aerosol influence mucosal immunity and chronic stress? A randomized controlled clinical trial. J. Physiol. Anthropol. **36**, 10 (2017). https://doi.org/10/gc5vqp
11. D. Huber, M. Mayr, A. Hartl, S. Sittenthaler, E. Traut-Mattausch, R. Weisböck-Erdheim, J. Freidl, Sustainability of hiking in combination with coaching in cardiorespiratory fitness and quality of life. Int. J. Environ. Res. Public Health. **19**, 3848 (2022). https://doi.org/10.3390/ijerph19073848
12. R. Chen, B. Hu, Y. Liu, J. Xu, G. Yang, D. Xu, C. Chen, Beyond PM2.5: the role of ultrafine particles on adverse health effects of air pollution. Biochim. Biophys. Acta. **1860**, 2844–2855 (2016). https://doi.org/10/f86rmb.
13. S. Costa, J. Ferreira, C. Silveira, C. Costa, D. Lopes, H. Relvas, C. Borrego, P. Roebeling, A.I. Miranda, J.P. Teixeira, Integrating health on air quality assessment—review report on health risks of two major European outdoor air pollutants: PM and NO_2. J. Toxicol. Environ. Health B Crit. Rev. **17**, 307–340 (2014). https://doi.org/10/gddk9h
14. B.A. Franklin, R. Brook, C. Arden Pope, Air pollution and cardiovascular disease. Curr. Probl. Cardiol. **40**, 207–238 (2015). https://doi.org/10/f69tdx
15. K.-H. Kim, E. Kabir, S. Kabir, A review on the human health impact of airborne particulate matter. Environ. Int. **74**, 136–143 (2015). https://doi.org/10/f6tsmq
16. R. Maheswaran, Air pollution and stroke—an overview of the evidence base. Spat. Spatiotemporal Epidemiol. **18**, 74–81 (2016). https://doi.org/10/gc8s4w
17. European Environment Agency: Air quality in Europe 2021 (2021). https://www.eea.europa.eu/publications/air-quality-in-europe-2021/
18. WHO: Burden of disease from environmental noise: quantification of healthy life years lost in Europe. World Health Organization, Regional Office for Europe, Copenhagen (2011). https://www.euro.who.int/__data/assets/pdf_file/0008/136466/e94888.pdf
19. A. Parajuli, M. Grönroos, N. Siter, R. Puhakka, H.K. Vari, M.I. Roslund, A. Jumpponen, N. Nurminen, O.H. Laitinen, H. Hyöty, J. Rajaniemi, A. Sinkkonen, Urbanization reduces transfer of diverse environmental microbiota indoors. Front Microbiol. **9**, 84 (2018). https://doi.org/10.3389/FMICB.2018.00084
20. J.H. O'Keefe, R. Vogel, C.J. Lavie, L. Cordain, Achieving hunter-gatherer fitness in the 21(st) century: back to the future. Am. J. Med. **123**, 1082–1086 (2010). https://doi.org/10/bbkhj4
21. R.R. Patil, Urbanization as a determinant of health: a socioepidemiological perspective. Soc. Work Public Health. **29**, 335–341 (2014). https://doi.org/10/gc5sc6
22. D. Ding, K.D. Lawson, T.L. Kolbe-Alexander, E.A. Finkelstein, P.T. Katzmarzyk, W. van Mechelen, M. Pratt, Lancet physical activity series 2 executive committee: the economic burden of physical inactivity: a global analysis of major non-communicable diseases. Lancet **388**, 1311–1324 (2016). https://doi.org/10/f84zsj
23. I.-M. Lee, E.J. Shiroma, F. Lobelo, P. Puska, S.N. Blair, P.T. Katzmarzyk, Impact of physical inactivity on the world's major non-communicable diseases. Lancet **380**, 219–229 (2012). https://doi.org/10/f2fthh

24. M. Soga, K.J. Gaston, Y. Yamaura, K. Kurisu, K. Hanaki, Both direct and vicarious experiences of nature affect children's willingness to conserve biodiversity. Int. J. Environ. Res. Public Health **13** (2016). https://doi.org/10/f8tbtk
25. C.A. Capaldi, R.L. Dopko, J.M. Zelenski, The relationship between nature connectedness and happiness: a meta-analysis. Front Psychol. **5** (2014). https://doi.org/10/gdcc28
26. J.M. Zelenski, E.K. Nisbet, Happiness and feeling connected: the distinct role of nature relatedness. Environ. . Behav. **46**, 3–23 (2014). https://doi.org/10/gdcc27
27. M. Rulle, W. Hoffmann, K. Kraft, K. Biehle, *Erfolgsstrategien im Gesundheitstourismus: Analyse zur Erwartung und Zufriedenheit von Gästen* (Schmidt, Berlin, 2010)
28. V. Leichtfried, C. Möller, M. Raggautz, W. Schobersberger, Evidenz-basierter Gesundheitstourismus. in *Qualitätsmanagement in Wellnesseinrichtungen Krczal*, ed. by A. Krczal, E. Krczal, K. Weiermair (Schmidt, Göttingen, 2011), pp. 155–168
29. G.C. Steckenbauer, S. Tischler, A. Hartl, C. Pichler, Destination and product development rested on evidence-based health tourism. in *The Routledge Handbook of Health Tourism*, ed. by M.K. Smith, L. Puczkó (Routledge, Taylor & Francis Group, New York, 2017), pp. 315–331
30. NCBI: PubMed, https://www.ncbi.nlm.nih.gov/pubmed/
31. AHCPR: Agency for Healthcare Research & Quality, https://www.ahrq.gov/
32. J. Doré, M.-C. Multon, J.-M. Béhier, Participants of giens XXXII, round table no. 2: the human gut microbiome as source of innovation for health: Which physiological and therapeutic outcomes could we expect? Therapie. **72**, 21–38 (2017). https://doi.org/10/gfgpcd
33. D.J. Jackson, J.E. Gern, R.F. Lemanske, Lessons learned from birth cohort studies conducted in diverse environments. J. Allergy Clin. Immunol. **139**, 379–386 (2017). https://doi.org/10/f9wxhp
34. I. Hanski, Biodiversity, microbes and human well-being. Ethics Sci. Environ. Polit. **14**, 19–25 (2014). https://doi.org/10/gfvjbt
35. M. Saleem, Microbiome community ecology: fundamentals and applications. Springer International Publishing (2015)
36. S. Whitmee, A. Haines, C. Beyrer, F. Boltz, A.G. Capon, B.F. de Souza Dias, A. Ezeh, H. Frumkin, P. Gong, P. Head, R. Horton, G.M. Mace, R. Marten, S.S. Myers, S. Nishtar, S.A. Osofsky, S.K. Pattanayak, M.J. Pongsiri, C. Romanelli, A. Soucat, J. Vega, D. Yach, Safeguarding human health in the anthropocene epoch: report of the rockefeller foundation–lancet commission on planetary health. The Lancet **386**, 1973–2028 (2015). https://doi.org/10/gbn6w4
37. T.S. Postler, S. Ghosh, Understanding the holobiont: how microbial metabolites affect human health and shape the immune system. Cell Metab. **26**, 110–130 (2017). https://doi.org/10.1016/j.cmet.2017.05.008
38. A. Parajuli, M. Gronroos, N. Siter, R. Puhakka, H.K. Vari, M.I. Roslund, A. Jumpponen, N. Nurminen, O.H. Laitinen, H. Hyoty, J. Rajaniemi, A. Sinkkonen, Urbanization reduces transfer of diverse environmental microbiota indoors. Front Microbiol. **9**, 84 (2018). https://doi.org/10/gc2p8d
39. S.L. Prescott, G. Wegienka, A.C. Logan, D.L. Katz, Dysbiotic drift and biopsychosocial medicine: how the microbiome links personal, public and planetary health. Biopsychosoc. Med. **12**, 7 (2018). https://doi.org/10/gfgpcg
40. B.L.K. Chawes, Low-grade disease activity in early life precedes childhood asthma and allergy. Dan. Med. J. **63**, (2016). PMID: 27477800
41. O.S. Von Ehrenstein, E. Von Mutius, S. Illi, L. Baumann, O. Böhm, R. von Kries, Reduced risk of hay fever and asthma among children of farmers. Clin. Exp. Allergy. **30**, 187–193 (2000). https://doi.org/10.1046/j.1365-2222.2000.00801.x
42. J. Riedler, C. Braun-Fahrländer, W. Eder, M. Schreuer, M. Waser, S. Maisch, D. Carr, R. Schierl, D. Nowak, E. von Mutius, Exposure to farming in early life and development of asthma and allergy: a cross-sectional survey. The Lancet **358**, 1129–1133 (2001). https://doi.org/10/bw9sv3
43. J. Riedler, W. Eder, G. Oberfeld, M. Schreuer, Austrian children living on a farm have less hay fever, asthma and allergic sensitization. Clin. Exp. Allergy **30**, 194–200 (2000). https://doi.org/10/bmzkms

44. F. Horak, M. Studnicka, C. Gartner, A. Veiter, E. Tauber, R. Urbanek, T. Frischer, Parental farming protects children against atopy: longitudinal evidence involving skin prick tests. Clin. Exp. Allergy. **32**, 1155–1159 (2002). https://doi.org/10.1046/j.1365-2745.2002.01448.x
45. A. Schulze, R.T.van. Strien, G. Praml, D. Nowak, K. Radon, Characterisation of asthma among adults with and without childhood farm contact. Eur. Respir. J. **29**, 1169–1173 (2007). https://doi.org/10/bvt9wx
46. K. Radon, V. Ehrenstein, G. Praml, D. Nowak, Childhood visits to animal buildings and atopic diseases in adulthood: an age-dependent relationship. Am. J. Ind. Med. **46**, 349–356 (2004). https://doi.org/10/frdtnd
47. A.P. Krueger, The biological effects of air ions. Int. J. Biometeorol. **29**, 205–6 (1985). https://doi.org/10/bf96wt
48. T. Alfvén, C. Braun-Fahrländer, B. Brunekreef, E. von Mutius, J. Riedler, A. Scheynius, M. van Hage, M. Wickman, M.R. Benz, J. Budde, K.B. Michels, D. Schram, E. Ublagger, M. Waser, G. Pershagen, PARSIFAL study group: Allergic diseases and atopic sensitization in children related to farming and anthroposophic lifestyle—the PARSIFAL study. Allergy. **61**, 414–421 (2006). https://doi.org/10/dzrcb9
49. M. Ege, M. Mayer, A.-C. Normand, J. Genuneit, W.O.C.M. Cookson, C. Braun-Fahrländer, D. Heederik, R. Piarroux, E. von Mutius, GABRIELA Transregio 22 study group: exposure to environmental microorganisms and childhood asthma. N. Engl. J. Med. **364**, 701–709 (2011). https://doi.org/10/cf639q
50. J. Kaiser, Immunology. How farm life prevents asthma. Science **349**, 1034 (2015). https://doi.org/10/gfvnc5
51. M. Ege, C. Bieli, R. Frei, R.T. van Strien, J. Riedler, E. Üblagger, D. Schram-Bijkerk, B. Brunekreef, M. van Hage, A. Scheynius, G. Pershagen, M.R. Benz, R. Lauener, E. von Mutius, C. Braun-Fahrländer, The PARSIFAL study team: prenatal farm exposure is related to the expression of receptors of the innate immunity and to atopic sensitization in school-age children. J. Allergy Clin. Immunol. **117**, 817–823 (2006). https://doi.org/10/d32pp2
52. E. von Mutius, D. Vercelli, Farm living: effects on childhood asthma and allergy. Nat. Rev. Immunol. **10**, 861–868 (2010). https://doi.org/10/bxc2h5
53. A. Dreyer, A. Menzel, Hiking tourism in Germany's low and high mountain regions. in *Mountain Tourism: Experiences, Communities, Environments and Sustainable Futures*, ed. by H. Richins, J.S. Hull (Cabi Publishing, Wallingford, Oxfordshire ; Boston, MA, 2016)
54. BMWI: Grundlagenuntersuchung Freiziet- und Urlaubsmarkt Wandern. Bundesministerium für Wirtschaft und Technologie, Berlin (2010)
55. M. Faulhaber, E. Pocecco, M. Niedermeier, G. Ruedl, D. Walter, R. Sterr, H. Ebner, W. Schobersberger, M. Burtscher, Fall-related accidents among hikers in the Austrian Alps: a 9-year retrospective study. BMJ Open Sport Exerc. Med. **3**, e000304 (2017). https://doi.org/10/gcrnd7
56. L. Butykova, J. Kolesar, A. Turecekova, S. Najvarova, Changes in the elimination of histamine, noradrenaline, adrenaline and vanilmandelic acid during high-mountain climatic therapy at Strbske Pleso. Fysiatricky a reumatologicky vestnik. **51**, 103–107 (1973). PMID: 4735215
57. Z. Cepilova, M. Porubska, J. Slamova, Climate therapy of uveitis in a mountain environment. Cesk. Oftalmol. **49**, 90–94 (1993). PMID: 8490974
58. C. Karagiannidis, G. Hense, B. Rueckert, P.Y. Mantel, B. Ichters, K. Blaser, G. Menz, C.B. Schmidt-Weber, High-altitude climate therapy reduces local airway inflammation and modulates lymphocyte activation. Scand. J. Immunol. **63**, 304–310 (2006). https://doi.org/10/dcgvpz
59. H.U. Simon, M. Grotzer, W.H. Nikolaizik, K. Blaser, M.H. Schoni, High altitude climate therapy reduces peripheral blood T lymphocyte activation, eosinophilia, and bronchial obstruction in children with house-dust mite allergic asthma. Pediatr. Pulmonol. **17**, 304–11 (1994). https://doi.org/10/dsnx2f
60. W.S. van Leeuwen, Bronchial asthma in relation to climate. Proc. R Soc. Med. **17**, 19–26 (1924). PMID: 19984206

61. M. Burtscher, O. Bachmann, T. Hatzl, B. Hotter, R. Likar, M. Philadelphy, W. Nachbauer, Cardiopulmonary and metabolic responses in healthy elderly humans during a 1-week hiking programme at high altitude. Eur. J. Appl. Physiol. **84**, 379–386 (2001). https://doi.org/10/ck5rdw
62. R.M. Leuschner, G. Boehm, Pollen and inorganic particles in the air of climatically very different places in switzerland. Grana. **20**, 161–167 (1981). https://doi.org/10/bjz52q
63. W. Schobersberger, V. Leichtfried, M. Mueck-Weymann, E. Humpeler, Austrian moderate altitude studies (AMAS): benefits of exposure to moderate altitudes (1500–2500 m). Sleep Breathing **14**, 201–207 (2010). https://doi.org/10/bpjhgq
64. H.D. Theiss, M.Adam, S. Greie, W. Schobersberger, E. Humpeler, W.-M. Franz, Increased levels of circulating progenitor cells after 1-week sojourn at moderate altitude (Austrian moderate altitude study II, AMAS II). Respir. Physiol. Neurobiol. **160**, 232–238 (2008). https://doi.org/10/bs5b3v
65. B. a Porta, J. Barandun, B. Wuthrich, Atopic neurodermatitis—therapy in high altitude climate. Praxis. **89**, 1147–53 (2000). PMID: 10959203
66. R. Engst, E. Vocks, High-mountain climate therapy for skin diseases and allergies—mode of action, therapeutic results, and immunologic effects. Rehabilitation (Stuttg) **39**, 215–222 (2000). https://doi.org/10/cw6kbd
67. L.H. Rijssenbeek-Nouwens, E.H. Bel, High-altitude treatment: a therapeutic option for patients with severe, refractory asthma? Clin. Exp. Allergy **41**, 775–782 (2011). https://doi.org/10/b35kb2
68. W. Schobersberger, P. Schmid, M. Lechleitner, S.P. von Duvillard, H. Hörtnagl, H.-C. Gunga, A. Klingler, , D. Fries, K. Kirsch, R. Spiesberger, R. Pokan, P. Hofmann, F. Hoppichler, G. Riedmann, H. Baumgartner, E. Humpeler, Austrian moderate altitude study 2000 (AMAS 2000). The effects of moderate altitude (1700 m) on cardiovascular and metabolic variables in patients with metabolic syndrome. Eur. J. Appl. Physiol. **88**, 506–514 (2003). https://doi.org/10/bqrrxb
69. E. Humpeler, W. Schobersberger, Das Forschungsprojekt AMAS 2000 sowie das Nachfolgeprojekt AMAS II: Chancen für den alpinen Gesundheitstourismus. (2008)
70. G. Neumayr, D. Fries, M. Mittermayer, E. Humpeler, A. Klingler, W. Schobersberger, R. Spiesberger, R. Pokan, P. Schmid, R. Berent, Effects of hiking at moderate and low altitude on cardiovascular parameters in male patients with metabolic syndrome: Austrian moderate altitude study. Wilderness Environ. Med. **25**, 329–34 (2014). https://doi.org/10/gdgz8c
71. E.D. Bowler, M.L. Buyung-Ali, M.T. Knight, S.A. Pullin, A systematic review of evidence for the added benefits to health of exposure to natural environments. BMC Public Health **10**, (2010). https://doi.org/10.1186/1471-2458-10-456
72. V.F. Gladwell, D.K. Brown, C. Wood, G.R. Sandercock, J.L. Barton, The great outdoors: how a green exercise environment can benefit all. Extrem. Physiol. Med. **2**, 3 (2013). https://doi.org/10/gfvsnz
73. M.J. Craig, C.A. Logan, L.S.Prescott, Natural environments, nature relatedness and the ecological theater: connecting satellites and sequencing to shinrin-yoku. J. Physiol. Anthropol. **35**, (2016). https://doi.org/10.1186/s40101-016-0083-9
74. M. Niedermeier, J. Einwanger, A.Hartl, M. Kopp, Affective responses in mountain hiking-A randomized crossover trial focusing on differences between indoor and outdoor activity. PLoS ONE. **12**, e0177719 (2017). https://doi.org/10/f974gn
75. M. Winklmayr, C. Kluge, W. Winklmayr, H. Küchenhoff, M. Steiner, M. Ritter, A. Hartl, Radon balneotherapy and physical activity for osteoporosis prevention: a randomized, placebo-controlled intervention study. Radiat. Environ. Biophys. **54**, 123–136 (2015). https://doi.org/10/f67hjq
76. W. Schobersberger, S. Greie, E. Humpeler, M. Mittermayr, D. Fries, B. Schobersberger, E. Artner-Dworzak, W. Hasibeder, A. Klingler, H.C. Gunga, Austrian moderate altitude study (AMAS 2000): erythropoietic activity and Hb-O(2) affinity during a 3-week hiking holiday at moderate altitude in persons with metabolic syndrome. High. Alt. Med. Biol. **6**, 167–77 (2005). https://doi.org/10/d9pdx3

77. W. Schobersberger, V. Leichtfried, M. Mueck-Weymann, E. Humpeler, Austrian moderate altitude studies (AMAS): benefits of exposure to moderate altitudes (1500–2500 m). Sleep Breath. **14**, 201–207 (2010). https://doi.org/10/bpjhgq
78. B. Schobersberger, W. Schobersberger, Präventivmedizinische und gesundheitstouristische Askpekte der mittleren Höhen. in *Alpin- und Höhenmedizin* F. Berghold, H. Brugger, M. Burtscher, W. Domej, B. Durrer, R. Fischer, P. Paal, W. Schaffert, W. Schobersberger, G. Sumann. (Springer, Berlin, Heidelberg 2019). https://doi.org/10.1007/978-3-662-56396-0
79. E.G. James, Short-term differential training decreases postural sway. Gait Posture **39**, 172–176 (2014). https://doi.org/10/f5khtq
80. J. Prossegger, D. Huber, C. Grafetstätter, C. Pichler, R. Weisböck-Erdheim, B. Iglseder, G. Wewerka, A. Hartl, Effects of moderate mountain hiking and balneotherapy on community-dwelling older people: a randomized controlled trial. Exp. Gerontol. **122**, 74–84 (2019). https://doi.org/10/gf3k7z
81. B. Orland, Alpine milk: dairy farming as a pre-modern strategy of land use. Environ. Hist. **10**, 327–364 (2004). https://doi.org/10/cf3wqt
82. F. Visioli, A. Strata, Milk, dairy products, and their functional effects in humans: a narrative review of recent evidence1. Adv. Nutr. **5**, 131–143 (2014). https://doi.org/10/f53bt7
83. C.B. Hauswirth, M.R.L. Scheeder, J.H. Beer, High omega-3 fatty acid content in Alpine cheese: the basis for an Alpine paradox. Circulation **109**, 103–107 (2004). https://doi.org/10/fw72kb
84. A. Lluis, M. Depner, B. Gaugler, P. Saas, V.I. Casaca, D. Raedler, S. Michel, J. Tost, J. Liu, J. Genuneit, P. Pfefferle, M. Roponen, J. Weber, C. Braun-Fahrländer, J. Riedler, R. Lauener, D.A. Vuitton, J.-C. Dalphin, J. Pekkanen, E. von Mutius, B. Schaub, Protection against allergy: study in rural environments study group: increased regulatory t-cell numbers are associated with farm milk exposure and lower atopic sensitization and asthma in childhood. J. Allergy Clin. Immunol. **133**, 551–559 (2014). https://doi.org/10/f2pvcd
85. T. Brick, Y. Schober, C. Böcking, J. Pekkanen, J. Genuneit, G. Loss, J.-C. Dalphin, J. Riedler, R. Lauener, W.A. Nockher, H. Renz, O. Vaarala, C. Braun-Fahrländer, E. von Mutius, M.J. Ege, P.I Pfefferle, A. Karvonen, P. Tiittanen, M.-L. Dalphin, B. Schaub, M. Depner, S. Illi, M. Kabesch, ω-3 fatty acids contribute to the asthma-protective effect of unprocessed cow's milk. J. Allergy Clin. Immunol. **137**, 1699–1706.e13 (2016). https://doi.org/10/f8q8wh
86. M. Waser, K.B. Michels, C. Bieli, H. Flöistrup, G. Pershagen, E. von Mutius, M. Ege, J. Riedler, D. Schram-Bijkerk, B. Brunekreef, M. van Hage, R. Lauener, C. Braun-Fahrländer, PARSIFAL study team: Inverse association of farm milk consumption with asthma and allergy in rural and suburban populations across Europe. Clin. Exp. Allergy **37**, 661–670 (2007). https://doi.org/10/fm2zbs
87. M.R. Perkin, D.P. Strachan, Which aspects of the farming lifestyle explain the inverse association with childhood allergy? J. Allergy Clin. Immunol. **117**, 1374–1381 (2006). https://doi.org/10/fq6zn5
88. C. Braun-Fahrländer, E. von Mutius, Can farm milk consumption prevent allergic diseases? Clin. Exp. Allergy **41**, 29–35 (2011). https://doi.org/10/fk9qbs
89. C. Munteanu, D. Munteanu, M. Hoteteu, G. Dogaru, Balneotherapy—medical, scientific, educational and economic relevance reflected by more than 250 articles published in Balneo Research Journal. Balneo Res. J. **10**, 174–203 (2019). https://doi.org/10.12680/balneo.2019.257
90. A. Fioravanti, M. Karagülle, T. Bender, M.Z. Karagülle, Balneotherapy in osteoarthritis: Facts, fiction and gaps in knowledge. European J. Integr. Med. **9**, 148–150 (2017). https://doi.org/10.1016/j.eujim.2017.01.001
91. Cochrane Library: Cochrane Reviews|Cochrane Library. https://www.cochranelibrary.com/. Accessed 2022/04/04
92. A.P. Verhagen, S.M.A. Bierma-Zeinstra, M. Boers, , J.R. Cardoso, J. Lambeck, R.A. de Bie, H.C.W. de Vet, Balneotherapy for osteoarthritis. Cochrane Database Syst. Rev. CD006864 (2007). https://doi.org/10/dmjz9h

93. A.P. Verhagen, S.M. Bierma-Zeinstra, M. Boers, J.R. Cardoso, J. Lambeck, R. de Bie, H.C. de Vet, Balneotherapy (or spa therapy) for rheumatoid arthritis. Cochrane Database Syst. Rev. (2015). https://doi.org/10.1002/14651858.CD000518.pub2
94. M.A. de M. Silva, L.C. Nakano, L.L. Cisneros, F.M. Jr, Balneotherapy for chronic venous insufficiency. Cochrane Database of Syst. Rev. (2019). https://doi.org/10.1002/14651858.CD013085.pub2
95. European Union (Interact): Project -. https://keep.eu/projects/18939/Trail-for-Health-Nord-EN/. Accessed 2022/04/04
96. C. Song, H. Ikei, Y. Miyazaki, Physiological effects of nature therapy: a review of the research in Japan. Int. J. Environ Res. Public Health **13**, (2016). https://doi.org/10/f82vpf
97. Q. Li, Effect of forest bathing trips on human immune function. Environ. Health Prev. Med. **15**, 9–17 (2010). https://doi.org/10/fskjk3
98. Y. Tsunetsugu, B. Park, Y. Miyazaki, Trends in research related to "Shinrin-yoku" (taking in the forest atmosphere or forest bathing) in Japan. Environ. Health Prev. Med. **15**, 27–37 (2010). https://doi.org/10/frmcfc
99. Y. Tsunetsugu, B.-J. Park, J. Lee, T. Kagawa, Y. Miyazaki, Psychological relaxation effect of forest therapy - results of field experiments in 19 forests in Japan involving 228 participants. Nippon Eiseigaku Zasshi (Japan. J. Hyg.). **66**, 670–676 (2011). https://doi.org/10/bp5wg4
100. H. Kamioka, K.Tsutani, Y. Mutoh, T. Honda, N. Shiozawa, S. Okada, S.-J. Park, J. Kitayuguchi, M. Kamada, H. Okuizumi, S. Handa, A systematic review of randomized controlled trials on curative and health enhancement effects of forest therapy. Psychol. Res. Behav. Manag. **5**, 85–95 (2012). https://doi.org/10/gd87wj
101. Association of Nature and Forest Therapy Guides and Programs. https://www.natureandforesttherapy.org/. Accessed 2019/03/25
102. B. Oh, K.J. Lee, C. Zaslawski, A. Yeung, D. Rosenthal, L. Larkey, M. Back, Health and wellbeing benefits of spending time in forests: systematic review. Environ. Health Prev. Med. **22**, 71 (2017). https://doi.org/10/gddmxb
103. G.X. Mao, Y. Cao, B. Wang, S. Wang, Z. Chen, J. Wang, W. Xing, X. Ren, X. Lv, J. Dong, S. Chen, X. Chen, G. Wang, J. Yan, The salutary influence of forest bathing on elderly patients with chronic heart failure. Int. J. Environ. Res. Public Health **14**, (2017). https://doi.org/10/gbmd7z
104. G.X. Mao, Y.B. Cao, Y. Yang, Z.M. Chen, J.H. Dong, S.S. Chen, Q. Wu, X.L. Lyu, B.B. Jia, J. Yan, G.F. Wang, Additive benefits of twice forest bathing trips in elderly patients with chronic heart failure. Biomed. Environ. Sci. **31**, 159–162 (2018). https://doi.org/10/gffk5n
105. C. Zeng, B. Lyu, S. Deng, Y. Yu, N. Li, W. Lin, D. Li, Q. Chen, Benefits of a three-day bamboo forest therapy session on the physiological responses of university students. IJERPH. **17**, 3238 (2020). https://doi.org/10.3390/ijerph17093238
106. J.-G. Kim, W.-S. Shin, Forest therapy alone or with a guide: is there a difference between self-guided forest therapy and guided forest therapy programs? IJERPH. **18**, 6957 (2021). https://doi.org/10.3390/ijerph18136957
107. A. Dolling, H. Nilsson, Y. Lundell, Stress recovery in forest or handicraft environments—an intervention study. Urban For. Urban Greening **27**, 162–172 (2017). https://doi.org/10/gctct6
108. U.K. Stigsdotter, S.S. Corazon, U. Sidenius, J. Kristiansen, P. Grahn, It is not all bad for the grey city—a crossover study on physiological and psychological restoration in a forest and an urban environment. Health Place **46**, 145–154 (2017). https://doi.org/10/gbvndw
109. F. Meneguzzo, L. Albanese, M. Antonelli, R. Baraldi, F. Becheri, F. Centritto, D. Donelli, F. Finelli, F. Firenzuoli, G. Margheritini, V. Maggini, S. Nardini, M. Regina, F. Zabini, L. Neri, Short-term effects of forest therapy on mood states: a pilot study. IJERPH. **18**, 9509 (2021). https://doi.org/10.3390/ijerph18189509
110. H.-J. Hermann, Greening the economy in the Alpine region: report on the state of the Alps : Alpine convention : Alpine signals—special edition 6 : executive summary. Permanent Secretariat of the Alpine Convention, Innsbruck (2017)
111. C. Song, H. Ikei, T. Kagawa, Y. Miyazaki, Effects of walking in a forest on young women. Int. J. Environ. Res. Public Health **16** (2019). https://doi.org/10/gbvndw

112. C. Pichler, J. Freidl, M. Bischof, M. Kiem, R. Weißböck-Erdheim, D. Huber, G. Squarra, P. Murschetz, Hartl, A., Mountain hiking vs. forest therapy: a study protocol of novel types of nature-based intervention. IJERPH. **19**, 3888 (2022). https://doi.org/10.3390/ijerph19073888
113. European Environment Agency: The Alpine region—Biodiversity, Energy and Water. , Copenhagen (2016)
114. ALPARC: Alparc—the Alpine Network of Protected Areas. http://alparc.org/
115. World Health Organization, Convention on Biological Diversity, United Nations Environment Programme: Connecting global priorities: biodiversity and human health: a state of knowledge review. (2015)
116. I.J. Harrison, P.A. Green, T.A. Farrell, D. Juffe-Bignoli, L. Sáenz, C.J. Vörösmarty, Protected areas and freshwater provisioning: a global assessment of freshwater provision, threats and management strategies to support human water security. Aquat. Conserv. Mar. Freshw Ecosystems **26**, 103–120 (2016). https://doi.org/10/f8xbgm
117. J. Terraube, Á. Fernández-Llamazares, M. Cabeza, The role of protected areas in supporting human health: a call to broaden the assessment of conservation outcomes. Curr. Opin. Environ. Sustain. **25**, 50–58 (2017). https://doi.org/10/gck9fh
118. I.D. Wolf, H.K. Stricker, G. Hagenloh, Outcome-focused national park experience management: transforming participants, promoting social well-being, and fostering place attachment. J Sustain Tourism **23**, 358–381 (2015). https://doi.org/10/gfvh9z
119. R.A. Fuller, K.N. Irvine, P. Devine-Wright, P.H. Warren, K.J. Gaston, Psychological benefits of greenspace increase with biodiversity. Biol. Lett. **3**, 390–394 (2007). https://doi.org/10/bfmsdm
120. L.J. Wolf, S. Zu Ermgassen, A. Balmford, M. White, N. Weinstein, Is variety the spice of life? an experimental investigation into the effects of species richness on self-reported mental well-being. PLoS ONE. **12**, e0170225 (2017). https://doi.org/10/gfvjbn
121. C. Liddicoat, P. Bi, M. Waycott, J. Glover, A.J. Lowe, P. Weinstein, Landscape biodiversity correlates with respiratory health in Australia. J. Environ. Manag. **206**, 113–122 (2018). https://doi.org/10/gcxv2s
122. R. Puhakka, R Pitkänen, P. Siikamäki, The health and well-being impacts of protected areas in Finland. J. Sustain. Tourism **25**, 1830–1847 (2017). https://doi.org/10/gc8znf
123. S. Beamon, A. Falkenbach, G. Fainburg, K. Linde, Speleotherapy for asthma. Cochrane Database Syst. Rev. CD001741 (2001). https://doi.org/10/bnhnkd
124. W. Gaus, H. Weber, Efficacy and safety of speleotherapy in children with asthma bronchiale. Phys. Med. Rehab. Kuror. **20**, 144–151 (2010). https://doi.org/10/brs4mn
125. A. Falkenbach, J. Kovacs, A. Franke, K. Jörgens, K. Ammer, Radon therapy for the treatment of rheumatic diseases—review and meta-analysis of controlled clinical trials. Rheumatol. Int. **25**, 205–210 (2005). https://doi.org/10/cbqrqw
126. U. Lange, G. Dischereit, I. Tarner, K. Frommer, E. Neumann, U. Müller-Ladner, B. Kürten, The impact of serial radon and hyperthermia exposure in a therapeutic adit on pivotal cytokines of bone metabolism in rheumatoid arthritis and osteoarthritis. Clin. Rheumatol. **35**, 2783–2788 (2016). https://doi.org/10/f883kn
127. A. Franke, L. Reiner, K.-L. Resch, Long-term benefit of radon spa therapy in the rehabilitation of rheumatoid arthritis: a randomised, double-blinded trial. Rheumatol. Int. **27**, 703–713 (2007). https://doi.org/10/c8wx3h
128. A. Franke, T. Franke, Long-term benefits of radon spa therapy in rheumatic diseases: results of the randomised, multi-centre IMuRa trial. Rheumatol. Int. **33**, 2839–2850 (2013). https://doi.org/10/gfwrhd
129. J.M. Kuciel-Lewandowska, L. Pawlik-Sobecka, S. Płaczkowska, I. Kokot, M. Paprocka-Borowicz, The assessment of the integrated antioxidant system of the body and the phenomenon of spa reaction in the course of radon therapy: A pilot study. Adv. Clin. Exp. Med. **27**, 1341–1346 (2018). https://doi.org/10/gfwrhf
130. D. Passali, G. Gabelli, G.C. Passali, R. Mösges, L.M. Bellussi, Radon-enriched hot spring water therapy for upper and lower respiratory tract inflammation. Otolaryngol. Pol. **71**, 8–13 (2017). https://doi.org/10/gcmvqx

131. P.F. Rühle, G. Klein, T. Rung, H. Tiep Phan, C. Fournier, R. Fietkau, U.S. Gaipl, B. Frey, Impact of radon and combinatory radon/carbon dioxide spa on pain and hypertension: results from the explorative RAD-ON01 study. Mod. Rheumatol. **29**, 165–172 (2019). https://doi.org/10/gfwrhg
132. L. Laakso, A. Hirsikko, T. Gronholm, M. Kulmala, A. Luts, T.E. Parts, Waterfalls as sources of small charged aerosol particles. Atmos. Chem. Phys. **7**, 2271–2275 (2007). https://doi.org/10/bb6snb
133. P. Kolarž, M. Gaisberger, P. Madl, W. Hofmann, M. Ritter, A. Hartl, Characterization of ions at Alpine waterfalls. Atmos. Chem. Phys. **12**, 3687–3697 (2012). https://doi.org/10/f3zm4h
134. A. Hartl, C. Grafetstaetter, J. Prosegger, P. Hahne, H. Braunschmid, M. Winklmayr, Health effects of Alpine waterfalls. in *Research in protected areas 5th Symposium*. 5, (2013), pp. 265–268
135. M. Gaisberger, R. Sanovic, H. Dobias, P. Kolarz, A. Moder, J. Thalhamer, A. Selimovic, I. Huttegger, M. Ritter, A. Hartl, Effects of ionized waterfall aerosol on pediatric allergic asthma. J. Asthma : official journal of the Association for the Care of Asthma. **49**, 830–8 (2012). https://doi.org/10/gc3khp
136. Hohe Tauern Health: Hohe Tauern Health | Allergikerhotels in Krimml—Hohe Tauern. https://hohe-tauern-health.at/de. Accessed 2022/04/02
137. G.C. Steckenbauer, S. Tischler, A. Hartl, C. Pichler, A model for developing evidence-based health tourism: the case of "Alpine health region Salzburg, Austria". in *Tourism, Health, Wellbeing and Protected Areas*. 69–81 (2018). https://doi.org/10/gfpnbg
138. P. Kolarz, M. Gaisberger, P. Madl, W. Hofmann, M. Ritter, A. Hartl, Characterization of ions at Alpine waterfalls. Atmos. Chem. Phys. **12**, 1–11 (2012)
139. T. Stöggl, C. Schwarzl, E.E. Muller, M. Nagasaki, J. Stoggl, M. Schonfelder, J. Niebauer, Alpine skiing as winter-time high-intensity training. Med. Sci. Sports Exerc. **49**, 1859–1867 (2017). https://doi.org/10/gfx6gm
140. E. Muller, M. Gimpl, S. Kirchner, J. Kroll, R. Jahnel, J. Niebauer, D. Niederseer, P. Scheiber, Salzburg skiing for the elderly study: influence of Alpine skiing on aerobic capacity, strength, power, and balance. Scand. J. Med. Sci. Sports. **21**(Suppl 1), 9–22 (2011). https://doi.org/10/cw9smn
141. F. Dela, D. Niederseer, W. Patsch, C. Pirich, E. Muller, J. Niebauer, Glucose homeostasis and cardiovascular disease biomarkers in older alpine skiers. Scand. J. Med. Sci. Sports. **21**(Suppl 1), 56–61 (2011). https://doi.org/10/cn9kdb
142. D. Niederseer, E. Ledl-Kurkowski, K. Kvita, W. Patsch, F. Dela, E. Mueller, J. Niebauer, Salzburg skiing for the elderly study: changes in cardiovascular risk factors through skiing in the elderly. Scand. J. Med. Sci. Sports **21**(Suppl 1), 47–55 (2011). https://doi.org/10/c577pn
143. D. Niederseer, E. Steidle-Kloc, M. Mayr, E.E. Muller, J. Cadamuro, W. Patsch, F. Dela, E. Muller, J. Niebauer, Effects of a 12-week alpine skiing intervention on endothelial progenitor cells, peripheral arterial tone and endothelial biomarkers in the elderly. Int. J. Cardiol. **214**, 343–7 (2016). https://doi.org/10/f8mpct
144. J.F. Kanh, J.C. Jouanin, E. Bruckert, C.Y. Guezennec, H. Monod, Physiological effects of downhill skiing at moderate altitude in untrained middle-aged men. Wilderness Environ. Med. **7**, 199–207 (1996). https://www.wemjournal.org/article/S1080-6032(96)71011-6/pdf
145. T. Stöggl, C. Schwarzl, E.E. Muller, M. Nagasaki, J. Stoggl, P. Scheiber, M. Schonfelder, J. Niebauer, A Comparison between Alpine skiing, cross-country skiing and indoor cycling on cardiorespiratory and metabolic response. J. Sports Sci. Med. **15**, 184–195 (2016)
146. P.J. Anderson, R.S. Bovard, M.H. Murad, T.J. Beebe, Z. Wang, Health status and health behaviors among citizen endurance Nordic skiers in the United States. BMC Res. Notes. **10**, 305 (2017). https://doi.org/10/gfx6gq
147. K.B. Nagle, Cross-country skiing injuries and training methods. Curr. Sports Med. Rep. **14**, 442–447 (2015). https://doi.org/10/gfx6gn
148. J.A. Laukkanen, T. Laukkanen, S.K. Kunutsor, Cross-country skiing is associated with lower all-cause mortality: A population-based follow-up study. Scand. J. Med. Sci. Sports (2017). https://doi.org/10/gfx6gp

149. P. Tosi, A. Leonardi, F. Schena, The energy cost of ski mountaineering: effects of speed and ankle loading. J. Sports Med. Phys. Fitness. **49**, 25–29 (2009). PMID: 19188892
150. M. Faulhaber, M. Flatz, H. Gatterer, W. Schobersberger, M. Burtscher, Prevalence of cardiovascular diseases among alpine skiers and hikers in the Austrian Alps. High Alt. Med. Biol. **8**, 245–52 (2007). https://doi.org/10/b8z3dj
151. K.F. Hjuler, B. Bay, [Mountain medicine—an introduction. I]. Ugeskr Laeger. 178, (2016)
152. S. Haslinger, D. Huber, D. Morawetz, C. Blank, J. Prossegger, T. Dünnwald, A. Koller, C. Fink, A. Hartl, W. Schobersberger, Feasibility of ski mountaineering for patients following a total knee arthroplasty: a descriptive field study. Int. J. Environ. Res. Public Health **16**, (2019). https://doi.org/10/gf3k7x
153. R.C. Browning, J.R. Modica, R. Kram, A. Goswami, The effects of adding mass to the legs on the energetics and biomechanics of walking. Med. Sci. Sports Exerc. **39**, 515–525 (2007). https://doi.org/10/bz6x4w
154. R.C. Browning, R.N. Kurtz, H. Kerherve, Biomechanics of walking with snowshoes. Sports Biomech. **11**, 73–84 (2012). https://doi.org/10/cwm84k
155. J.N. Morris, A.E. Hardman, Walking to health. Sports Med. **23**, 306–32 (1997). https://doi.org/10/c688sg
156. A. Gupta, P.K. Sharma, V.K. Garg, A.K. Singh, S.C. Mondal, Role of serotonin in seasonal affective disorder. Eur. Rev. Med. Pharmacol. Sci. **17**, 49–55 (2013). PMID: 23329523
157. S. Greie, E. Humpeler, H.C. Gunga, E. Koralewski, A. Klingler, M. Mittermayr, D. Fries, M. Lechleitner, H. Hoertnagl, G. Hoffmann, G. Strauss-Blasche, W. Schobersberger, Improvement of metabolic syndrome markers through altitude specific hiking vacations. J. Endocrinol. Invest. **29**, 497–504 (2006). https://doi.org/10/gdgz8j
158. J. Mair, A. Hammerer-Lercher, M. Mittermayr, A. Klingler, E. Humpeler, O. Pachinger, W. Schobersberger, 3-week hiking holidays at moderate altitude do not impair cardiac function in individuals with metabolic syndrome. Int. J. Cardiol. **123**, 186–188 (2008). https://doi.org/10/chnf5g

Open Access This chapter is licensed under the terms of the Creative Commons Attribution 4.0 International License (http://creativecommons.org/licenses/by/4.0/), which permits use, sharing, adaptation, distribution and reproduction in any medium or format, as long as you give appropriate credit to the original author(s) and the source, provide a link to the Creative Commons license and indicate if changes were made.

The images or other third party material in this chapter are included in the chapter's Creative Commons license, unless indicated otherwise in a credit line to the material. If material is not included in the chapter's Creative Commons license and your intended use is not permitted by statutory regulation or exceeds the permitted use, you will need to obtain permission directly from the copyright holder.

KPI for Data-Driven Assessment of Innovative Development Paths for Nature-Based Health Tourism in the Alpine Region

Michael Bischof and Arnulf J. Hartl

Abstract Tourism has been one of the most important economic sectors in the Alps for many years. However, not least because of the cuts due to the pandemic, new and innovative approaches are needed to meet current challenges such as climate change, shortage of skilled workers or demographic change in order to make Alpine tourism fit for the future. The topic of health offers great potential in this context. With the KPI approach, therefore, a possible access to a nature-based health tourism with medical evidence is presented, which should support the actors from the tourism practice in the further development of the Alpine tourism. At the same time, the KPI approach also offers possibilities to enable an overall more sustainable development of the Alpine region. This paper places the KPI approach in a larger development framework and explains the underlying analytical system based on selected indicators.

Keywords Health tourism · Nature-based health tourism · Evidence · Sustainable development · Product development · Key performance indicators · Alpine region

1 Introduction

Tourism has been one of the most important drivers of prosperity and regional development in the Alpine region for decades. After years of growth driving not only income but also, among other things, the cost of living for locals, environmental problems, and cultural alienation, these and other problems and challenges have recently become apparent, not least because of the Covid pandemic [1–5]. During this time, it has also become apparent that the tourism industry is extremely vulnerable to these multiple challenges, which are primarily economic [6], but also environmental and socio-cultural.

Current consequences include increased planning uncertainty for companies, the associated loss of income, and an increasing migration of workers to other sectors [7]—whereby these effects are mutually reinforcing. From an economic point of

---

M. Bischof (✉) · A. J. Hartl
Institute of Ecomedicine, Paracelsus Medical University Salzburg, Salzburg, Austria
e-mail: michael.bischof@pmu.ac.at

© The Authors(s) 2023
D. Spoladore et al. (eds.), *Digital and Strategic Innovation for Alpine Health Tourism*,
SpringerBriefs in Applied Sciences and Technology,
https://doi.org/10.1007/978-3-031-15457-7_2

view, this has a doubly negative impact. On the one hand, the real income in the tourism industry decreases; on the other hand, the tax revenues in the region. This development is intensified by a growing seasonality, which increasingly fluctuates between a failing winter season and a (regional) crowded summer season, recording new lows and highs in arrivals and overnight stays [8]. Overtourism, meanwhile, has shifted from metropolitan areas to natural areas, which also has a double negative impact from an ecological point of view. On the one hand, the problem of individual mobility is shifting to regions that are even less prepared for it; on the other hand, the sensitive natural areas are suffering from the larger number of guests and their partly inappropriate behavior.

Sustainable tourism is one of the central development goals for the Alpine region [9, 10], but currently this goal is far away—even if there are already numerous positive examples, the overall picture is rather unsustainable [11, 12].

A possible approach for more sustainability in the tourism development of the Alps can be seen in the field of health [13]. Today, health is already a global megatrend [14]. And that this trend can also stand for an overarching development perspective is shown by the fact that the current discussion on the topic is increasingly less about the small-scale consideration of an individual and more about a holistic view [15]. Individual symptoms cannot be viewed in isolation from the rest of the body. And the body itself is also integrated into a superordinate system. The frame of reference for individual health is becoming increasingly complex. It is no longer just a matter of individual responsibility, but of a complex interplay of effects that are beyond the individual's control in many areas. This holistic concept of OneHealth links human health with the health of the environment [16]—right up to the global level.

With the pandemic, the importance of individuals, as well as general health, has become a key resource. This is increasingly reflected in the tourism sector. Travelers are looking for health-promoting forms of vacation, especially in nature, and hosts are experiencing a new counter value to the economy. An example of such forms of offer and, at the same time, one of the most innovative fields of development in tourism is nature-based health tourism based on medical evidence. Here, tourism offers with proven health effects (evidence) are created on the basis of natural, alpine resources [17, 18]. Although this market segment has played only a minor role in tourism to date, at the same time it holds a great potential in terms of a sustainable diversification of Alpine tourism.

2 The KPI-Based Approach

The Key Performance Indicators (KPI) approach presented here is intended to enhance the understanding of the development potential of the Alps in terms of nature-based health tourism with medical evidence and so help regions to valorize this potential. On the one hand, this is done by transferring knowledge from research to practice about the meaning and use of the underlying indicators of the KPI approach. The basic building of awareness of the need for sustainable tourism still represents an essential aspect. On the other hand, the KPI approach can also be used to identify very specific development paths in the form of target group-specific offers for nature-based health tourism with medical evidence, adapted to the respective regional characteristics of the Alpine regions.

To assess this potential, the KPI approach uses current scientific findings on the health effects of natural resources, as well as a number of indicators that are relevant in terms of basic tourism development. The indicators of the KPI approach can be divided into five main categories. The two main categories are "Natural Resources" and "Services" (economic resources). In addition, basic "Tourism Key Figures", information on "Image & Attractions" as well as on "Cooperation & Networks" of the region are used for the analysis. Medical evidence is integrated into this approach via the assignment to the natural resources as well as the services. How exactly this assignment happens will be explained in more detail later in this chapter.

Overall, this approach can be seen as an element for the development of sustainable tourism in the Alpine region. Although nature-based health tourism with medical is currently a niche market in tourism, it still has high growth potential and equally good growth opportunities [19, 20]. This is not least due to the increasing health awareness among the population, which has been growing for years and has received a further boost as a result of the pandemic [21]. Furthermore, this form of tourism already offers many starting points for addressing specific sustainability goals due to its structure. Existing forms of supply show that many of the challenges described can at least be actively addressed and thus either mitigated or even avoided altogether [12]. Moreover, this form of tourism offers additional opportunities for sustainable development, for example, with regard to occupational health care or socially relevant public health issues. Based on the three dimensions of sustainability—economy, ecology, social—and its derived Sustainable Development Goals (SDGs) [22], the KPI approach can be used to support, among others, the following goals in the context of Alpine tourism development.

- **Goal 3**: Ensure healthy lives and promote well-being for all at all ages
  - Creation of new, nature-based health offers that not only serve classic vacation motives such as recreation or adventure, but also provide socially relevant added value in the form of health (prevention, therapy, rehabilitation) that can be used by guests and locals alike.
  - Creation of health-oriented innovations by changing the perspective on the topics of health and vacation. Health moves to the center of attention, and experiencing nature and outdoor activities gain a new, concrete value through measurable health effects.
- **Goal 8**: Promote sustained, inclusive, and sustainable economic growth, full and productive employment, and decent work for all
  - Strengthening of alpine tourism through the creation of innovative forms of offers and the associated increase in quality as well as further differentiation and expansion of offers in the direction of health.

- Creation of new or protection of existing jobs in the cross-sectional area of tourism and health and, associated with this, an increase in the attractiveness as a place to live and work in Alpine regions, especially for well-educated young people.
- Expansion of existing or creation of new, regionally anchored value chains in the field of health.

- **Goal 15**: Protect, restore and promote sustainable use of terrestrial ecosystems, sustainably manage forests, combat desertification, and halt and reverse land degradation and halt biodiversity loss

    - Raising awareness of the value of nature by creating new, measurable value for natural resources through the topic of health.
    - Increasing the protection of natural resources or entire ecosystems by attributing value to health on the one hand and the need for healthy nature as the basis for economical use on the other.
    - Creation of control instruments for visitor guidance in the natural area by embedding nature use/activities in fixed value chains.

In this way, the abstract entity of the idea of sustainability results in concrete added values in a regional context. One could also speak of a kind of nature- and community-based health tourism.

However, the KPI approach must be viewed as one part of an overall process that additionally requires both upstream and downstream activities. Tourism product development, and thus in principle destination development, can be divided into four superordinate process steps. At the beginning there is the basic intention of further development (initial phase). This should be done with the broadest possible consensus among all regional stakeholders from politics, administration, business, and society. This primarily strategic step is followed by an analysis phase in which, among other things, the current status, existing challenges, and open potentials are surveyed. Based on this, suitable target groups for further development can be identified in a synthesis phase, under consideration of current trends, for example. With the help of these findings, the fourth step can finally be the concrete product development and market launch (product realization phase). The KPI approach can be located in this context as the link between the analysis and synthesis phases, which defines the framework of the analysis and supports the acting persons in the development. The KPIs are to be understood as a set of indicators that are used as a basis for assessing and analyzing the current situation of a region with regard to its development potential for nature-based health tourism with medical evidence and, finally, for identifying possible development paths for specific target groups based on indications. This supply-side analysis is integrated into a more comprehensive analysis that also considers the demand side, i.e., the perspective of the guests. This is done by a continuous guest survey in the Alpine region on expectations and needs. Also, in preparation for the downstream product development, socio-cultural characteristics of the region, e.g., customs, traditions, or special agricultural products, are considered. Through this extension of the analysis, on the one hand, the market potential for the potential

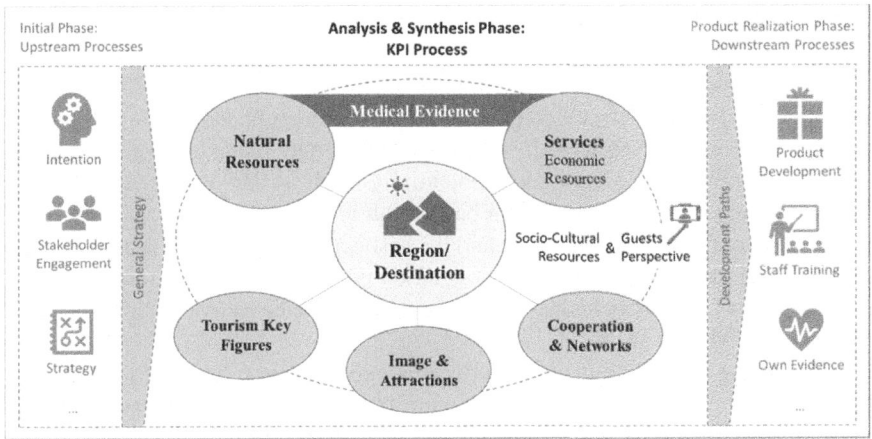

Fig. 1 Schematic overview of the KPI approach *source* authors

development paths can be better estimated, and, on the other hand, the regional anchoring of the products can be promoted. Figure 1 shows the KPI approach in a schematic overview.

The actual analysis of the regional potential for nature-based health tourism with medical evidence is done in several steps. First, health-promoting combinations of indicators are defined for the included indications on the basis of scientific findings. Thus, a data-driven evaluation of the individual indications is conducted. In this context, the indications represent the health-seeking target groups, e.g., guests who suffer from back pain and look for suitable tourism offers. In order to distinguish the appropriate combinations of indicators with respect to the different target groups, each indicator is assigned a value between 1 and 10, and this value may change depending on the importance of the indicator in terms of health impact for a target group. In this way, theoretically optimal combinations of important (health-promoting) and unimportant (health-neutral) indicators are obtained for each target group, so-called optimal conditions. These optimal conditions are taken as fixed for a certain period of time but must be adjusted at regular intervals to reflect new research findings. This applies in particular to the evaluation of natural resources and services. In a next step, the actual conditions, i.e., the individual indicators, are surveyed in the region to be analyzed. A specially developed questionnaire is used for this purpose. Values between 1 and 10 are then assigned to the collected data with the help of defined conversions, depending on the characteristics of the data. This is followed by a comparison of these values of the indicators, which represent the real conditions in the region, with the previously defined optimal conditions (benchmarking). In this way, the existing framework conditions in the respective region are analyzed with regard to the needs of the defined target groups and, finally, the theoretically most suitable target groups for the region are identified on the basis of the surveyed framework conditions. The result of this analysis is made available to the region in the form of texts and graphics. The meaning and the possible use of each indicator for the development of offers for the theoretically most suitable target group will be explained. In addition, the development paths identified in this way are placed in the context of nature-based health tourism and information is provided on the current state of scientific research (evidence) regarding the recommended combination of natural resources and services. In this way, the regions receive a comprehensive overview of their basic development potential as well as the significant indicators (KPI) for nature-based health tourism based with medical evidence.

The KPI approach described here and the associated analysis and synthesis steps form the core of an automated, ontology-based decision support system for alpine health tourism [23, 24], which was developed as a collaborative design approach within the HEALPS2 project.

In the following, the indicators behind the superordinate categories of the KPI approach are presented and, for a selection of the indicators, their relevance for the development of nature-based health offers is explained. First, the focus is on the two main categories of the approach, "Natural Resources" and "Services". Then, the three remaining categories, "Tourism Key Figures", "Image & Attractions" and "Cooperations & Networks" are examined in more detail.

2.1 Natural Resources and Services

There are already a large number of studies that confirm or at least suggest numerous health effects of natural resources at different levels of evidence (see also [25]). Starting with training for professional athletes [26], the development of the immune system in early childhood [27, 28], the findings also cover various groups of people specifically relevant to tourism, such as couples or the 65+ generation [29]. There is still a great need for research in this area, but for some indications such as allergies, overweight, lack of fitness, back pain, respiratory diseases, cardiovascular diseases, as well as stress and burnout, there are sufficient good findings to develop high-quality tourism offers. For the KPI approach, the following natural resources are considered by default:

- Alpine healing waters/thermal water,
- Alpine water—blue space (e.g., rivers, lakes, glaciers),
- Kneipp,
- Waterfalls,
- Forest,
- High altitude (>2500 m),
- Moderate altitude (1000–2500 m),
- Protected areas,
- Alpine farming,
- Radon treatment,
- Honey,
- Alpine milk & dairy products,

- Alpine plants/Phytotherapy,
- Healing cave/tunnel (Heilstollen),
- Moor.

Looking at the way in which natural resources develop their health effects, two types can be distinguished in principle. On the one hand, there are resources that can be characterized as having active health effects. On the other hand, there are those whose health effects can be described as passive. This means that active resources have an effect primarily due to their presence, e.g., radon. Passive resources can also have a positive health effect on their own, but they primarily only define a framework that stands for a health potential fundamentally included in it, such as a mountain. This distinction becomes clearer when changing the viewing angle, away from the natural resource to the user. From the user's point of view, these activity levels are reversed. In order to be able to access the health potential of a passive natural resource, the user must be active himself. For example, when hiking on a mountain. With an active natural resource, on the other hand, it is sufficient for the user to have simple, passive contact with the resource, such as in a radon-filled healing tunnel. However, the boundaries between these two types are fluid, depending on the objective or indication, because in reality, the resources do not always work separately from each other but together. An example of this is alpine air, which has just as much influence on the user in almost every use of another natural resource as the resource actually used. Nevertheless, this distinction helps in the evaluation of the respective natural resources with regard to the development of indication-specific, nature-based, and health-promoting tourism offers (e.g., alternation of exercise and relaxation) and likewise with a suitable target group approach (e.g., active vs. relaxation vacation). Table 1 shows a selection of natural alpine resources and their characterization in terms of their potential health effects. More detailed information on the effects of the individual resources can be found in this book in the article by Pichler et al. [25].

Thinking further about the use of natural resources for tourism, there is also a need for a range of services or activities that directly promote the intended health effect (e.g., treatments) or indirectly support it (e.g., advice). Depending on the

Table 1 Characterization of natural alpine resources as a basis for the development of nature-based health tourism offers (own selection and characterization)

Natural resource/activity	Resource character
Alpine farming & Alpine pastures	More active
Alpine milk & dairy products	More active
Forest/forest therapy	More passive
Healing waters/balneotherapy	More active
High & moderate altitude	More passive
Protected areas & biodiversity	More active
Speleotherapy/radon therapy	More active
Waterfalls	More active
Winter activities	More passive

target group, different combinations of health- and recreation-promoting services and activities can be used. Within the framework of the KPI approach presented here, the following services or activities are considered by default:

- Health Manager,
- Health check before & after,
- Courses in sport and exercise,
- Gymnastics/Balance training,
- Courses/services for relaxation,
- Massages,
- Physiotherapy,
- Nutritional advice,
- Meditation,
- Yoga,
- Guided hiking,
- Hiking,
- Climbing/Outdoor bouldering,
- (Nordic)Walking,
- Winter—snow-based activities,
- Winter—not snow-based activities,
- Cosmetics/Beauty offers,
- Spa treatments,
- Barrier-free,
- Car-free destination,
- Bicycle or E-Bike availability (e.g., rental or charging service).

Overall, offers of nature-based and health-promoting tourism are thus based on scientific knowledge (evidence) about the health effects of certain activities (e.g., hiking) in a natural environment (e.g., forest). And the basis is always a combination of natural resources and specific activities or services. It is advisable to combine several natural resources and activities, which are adapted to the target group to be addressed, not only in terms of the health effect, but also with regard to the attractiveness of the offer. All in all, high-quality but not necessarily high-priced offers can be created in this way, which fulfill the principles of sustainable tourism in many ways. In addition to a strong focus on cross-sectoral regional value chains, a high level of awareness for nature and health among guests and locals can also contribute to this. This can lead to a more sustainable use of resources and thus, for example, to the long-term preservation of nature as the basis for this type of economy.

2.2 Tourism Key Figures

Tourism is linked to numerous other economic sectors through complex interdependencies. This makes it difficult to calculate the generated added value precisely.

Nevertheless, the economic significance of tourism in general for a region or an individual destination can be measured and evaluated with the help of tourism indicators [30]. These indicators include, for example, the number of arrivals, the number of overnight stays, and the number and quality of existing accommodation facilities and available beds. These indicators, furthermore, can be used to derive other indicators for evaluating tourism, such as the average duration of stay or tourism intensity. The following indicators from this category are considered as part of the KPI approach:

- Number of inhabitants,
- Number of arrivals,
- Number of overnight stays,
- Distribution of guests among the 4 seasons,
- Source markets,
- Average age of tourists,
- Share of women among tourists,
- Duration of stay (DoS = overnight stays/arrivals),
- Tourism intensity ((TI = (overnight stays/inhabitants) * 1000)).

Tourism intensity is a key indicator for assessing local tourism. Basically, the more, the more important tourism is for the destination. However, this is only an economic indicator that does not allow any conclusions to be drawn about the ecological or socio-cultural carrying capacity of the region. In this respect, also environmental (ecological footprint) and socio-cultural (social carrying capacity) indicators should always be used when assessing tourism intensity. With regard to the development of offers in the segment of nature-based and health-promoting tourism, tourism intensity can also be an indirect indicator of the suitability of the region/destination for a certain target group. This is because tourism intensity can also indicate the social and psychological stress associated with tourism [31].

The average duration of stay indicates how long a guest stays in a region on average. This key figure therefore allows conclusions to be made on, among other things, the type of vacation and the type of guests [32]. In addition, the average duration of stay is also an important indicator from a business point of view, as it allows to calculate the bed occupancy rate in an accommodation company [30]. In the context of nature-based and health-promoting offers, the average duration of stay can also be of great importance since the expected health effect is often directly linked to the length of the stay. In this context, health can be seen as a good way to increase the average duration of stay in a region. On the one hand, this can be done by credibly demonstrating a higher health effect during a longer stay at a stretch. On the other hand, there is also the possibility to generate health improvements for the guests over a longer period in several stages, e.g., over three weekends per year, and thus bind the guests longer to the destination.

Another indicator for assessing tourism in a region can be seen in the origin of guests. Basically, within the tourism industry, one aim is to diversify the source markets with not too high shares in only one or two markets. On the one hand, in order to avoid being too economically dependent on just one or two markets. On the other hand, however, also in order to be able to address a sufficient number of potential guests throughout the entire year and at different seasons [33]. Covid-19 and the Russia-Ukraine conflict have softened this rule somewhat, as it is/was sometimes only possible to address domestic travelers, or entire markets have broken away completely. Nevertheless, a high degree of diversification should be considered in the source market analysis. In the future, one possible focus could be on source markets from which the Alps are also easily accessible by land (car, train).

Seasonality also plays an important role in tourism. In the interests of sustainable development of tourist destinations, the aim is to achieve a balanced distribution of guests throughout the year. Among other things, this provides greater planning security for operators and thus also for employees [34]. Nature-based and health-promoting tourism can in principle be seen as a year-round tourism. However, depending on the target group, seasonal differences in the distribution of these offers are reasonable. This can be related to the conditions of use or the availability of the underlying natural resources on the one hand and to the demand behavior of potential guests on the other hand.

Likewise, socio-demographic characteristics such as age or gender of current and potential guests are important for the design of offers. This applies on the one hand to the exact design of the offers and on the other hand to the marketing. Therefore, information about the possible target groups should already be available in advance because only then a targeted and, at the same time, market-tailored offer development can take place. Examples of the significance of socio-demographic characteristics with regard to different target groups (indications) are the burnout syndrome (related indications: burnout, chronic fatigue, severe stress) and back pain. For example, the following Figs. 2 and 3 show how the level of suffering of those affected changes with age and gender.

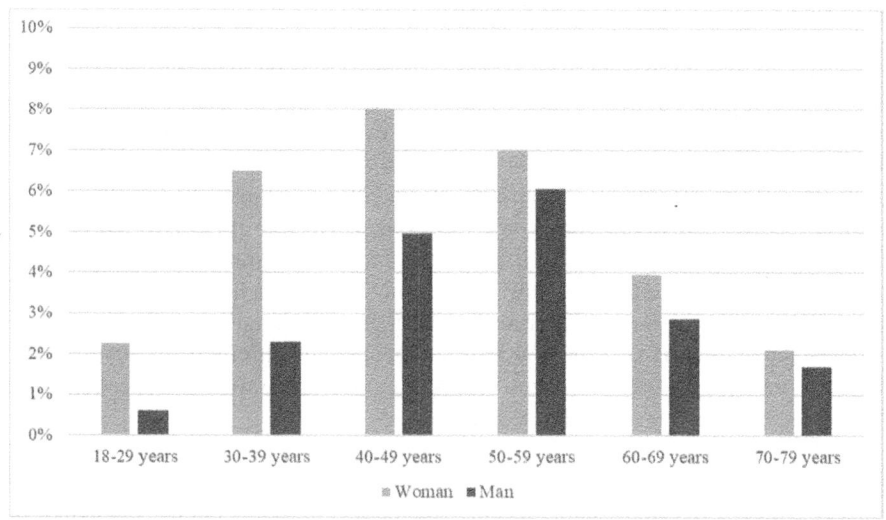

Fig. 2 Lifetime prevalence of burnout syndrome in Germany 2014 [35]

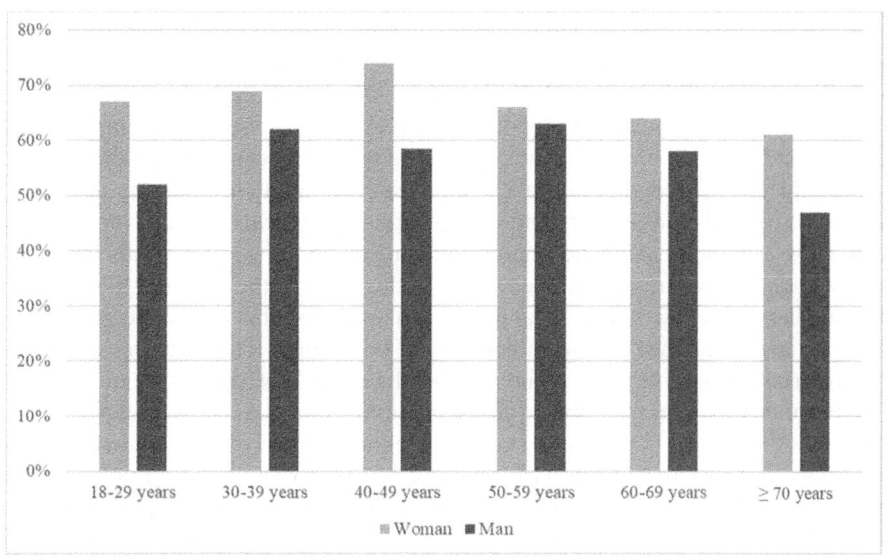

Fig. 3 Proportion of adults with back pain within the last twelve months by gender and age in Germany 2020 [36]

2.3 Image and Attractions

The image of a tourist region plays an increasingly important role in the choice of a destination by the guests [37]. Thereby, the image is significantly influenced by the most important unique selling propositions (USP) and attractions. Therefore, when developing and marketing offers in the segment of nature-based and health-promoting tourism, it should also make sure that the core values of the product are also reflected in the region as a whole. A correspondingly suitable image should therefore also be used specifically for the marketing of nature-based and health-promoting products. For target groups seeking health, the image can be an important reason for booking. In addition to the fundamental combinations of natural resources and services, the topics of air, light and noise pollution in particular offer very good approaches for the further development of a healthy image for destinations in the Alpine region. The period of time since a destination has been associated with health can also be used for a product marketing campaign. For example, a long tradition of health can be positioned as a quality attribute for health-promoting tourism. New, health-oriented aspects of the image can also be marketed as an innovative and timely development of the destination's own strengths. In the case that the unique selling proposition of a destination has a direct connection to nature, this should be used in the overall destination image, but especially in the external presentation of nature-based and health-promoting offers.

Finally, the tourist image is also related to the expectations of the guests. In this context, authenticity is increasingly seen as a quality feature in tourism. However, authenticity has not been defined uniformly in tourism science to date. Rather, there are several levels of authenticity. For example, a distinction is made between objective, constructive and existential authenticity [38]. An in-depth discussion of this challenge for tourism will not be conducted here, but rather some fundamental aspects in this context should be pointed out. Authenticity can be seen, among other things, as the subjective perception of a place, an attraction, or an encounter by the guest, who is increasingly looking for genuine and regionally typical offers and interactions [39]. How exactly an authentic impression is made on the guest depends on his or her individual expectations and ideas [40]. In this respect, the image of the destination and the marketing of individual products play an essential role in the generation of expectations and thus for the authenticity of your offers. Therefore, regardless of one's own assessment of product authenticity, the guests' perceptions should be evaluated regularly in order to be able to adjust possible differences between expectations and perceived reality. In principle, staged authenticity is part of tourism. In the sense of genuine and regionally typical experiences, however, it should be ensured that the staging does not have a purely touristic character and that the locals can also identify well with it, independently of an economic interest. This includes, among other things, also the real estate market, which should not focus on chalet investments, but on affordable and good housing for the local population in the future. After all, authenticity can only be created if the locals can both afford to live locally and at the same time really identify with the tourist offers. In this respect, it is important to think about offers that appeal equally to guests and locals and thereby automatically create shared moments between travelers and tourists. The question of authenticity is also a good example of the corrective potential of partnerships and networks. Within the KPI approach, the following indicators are considered from the Image & Attractions category:

- Unique selling proposition (USP),
- Attractions,
- Authenticity,
- Tourism image,
- Health tourism image,
- Tradition in health tourism.

2.4 Cooperation and Networks

Cooperation is important for the successful development of the destination as a whole as well as for the implementation of individual tourism products. Cooperations also play an important role for a successful and lasting establishment on the market [41]. Depending on the development phase as well as on the product orientation, there are variously important cooperation partners. Here it is important to form, maintain and further develop appropriate structures—e.g., through joint products.

Since tourism is to be understood as a cross-sectional industry, cooperations in the most diverse constellations are important. On the one hand, within the tourism sector itself, e.g., between destination management, hotels, and tour guides. On the other hand, however, also beyond the own branch borders, e.g., between hotels, craftsmen, agriculture, and the creative industries. With the focus on health tourism, innovative forms of cooperation between tourism and the health industry are also particularly important. These, but also the other forms of cooperation, represent an essential success factor. In principle, these cooperations can be local, regional, national, or international. In addition to these primarily content-oriented partnerships, good relations with administrative units such as state authorities and politics are also advantageous. For the KPI approach, the following indicators are analyzed from this category:

- Cooperation between stakeholders in the tourism industry,
- Cooperation between actors from different sectors (cross-sectoral cooperation),
- Cooperation with medical service providers,
- Cooperation with authorities and politics,
- Network participation (regional, national, international),
- Experience in projects,
- Share of regional food.

The cooperation with authorities and politics represents an important framework for the tourism development of a region [42]. In this context, the approach of nature-based and health-promoting tourism should be defined as a common and long-term goal of cooperation in the sense of economically beneficial and at the same time socially fair and ecologically responsible regional development. Best practices show that the establishment of a regional habitat management can be a viable option [43]. Here, ecological, as well as economic and social issues, can be addressed with the involvement of all stakeholders, and suitable solutions for the region can be developed. There are also examples that show how public–private partnerships can contribute to the positive development of nature-based and health-promoting tourism [44]. And finally, innovative approaches that integrate co-financed health prevention into tourism products could be developed in cooperation with politics.

Good cooperation within the tourism industry (e.g., in product development) can also lead, for example, to joint programs for employee retention, e.g., through the joint use of health-promoting offerings. Overall, cooperative behavior among all tourism stakeholders can contribute to both a higher quality of offerings and a better working climate within the industry [41]. This is therefore also important with regard to the attractiveness of employers, e.g., due to seasonal fluctuations, as well as the fundamental challenges of finding good employees.

Cooperation with partners from other industries is important in the context of the development of a nature-based and health-promoting tourism, in order to be able to develop and offer regionally anchored products with differentiated contents. Therefore, targeted partnerships should be sought that complement tourism offering with regionally authentic content, such as regional food, regional crafts, or other regional services. Examples of regionally-based product development in this area include organized tastings of regional products and visits to small-scale productions (e.g., show dairies). And especially the area of health-promoting tourism offers innovative cooperation opportunities, such as the local bakery developing special offers for people with diabetes.

Regional value chains can therefore contribute to success in tourism in many ways. On the one hand, industries within the region that are not directly involved in tourism can also benefit. On the other hand, it can also serve the guests' wishes for more authenticity and local resonance. This is particularly important against the background of a changing value system in society since, among other things, these values are becoming more and more important and are thus becoming an increasingly important part of the vacation. In this respect, these topics can also be used specifically for marketing purposes. The use of regional foods is a good example of this trend. Further examples, which can be important also for the guests, are among other things the topics of customs and handicrafts. A possible implementation idea is the integration of these aspects into existing services. For example, a breakfast buffet can be used as a "performance show" of regional agriculture/farmers. This could also be combined with a direct linking of the offered products to the producers. Also, the transfer of knowledge about the partnership, local traditions, and production methods can be exciting for the guests.

One possibility to improve the cooperation with different partners and thus also the own level of knowledge, as well as the innovative power, is the active participation in networks. Regional networks are particularly important for successful and sustainable development. Therefore, participation in regional networks should be actively forced. Among other things, ideas for your own product development can be generated, and open questions around the topic of nature-based and health-promoting tourism can be discussed and improved in a regional context. This is because regional networks strengthen small-scale market structures and thus increase the resilience of the region to future challenges such as climate or demographic change. National networks can be important, especially with regard to national strategies, e.g., in the area of funding, as well as current legislation. At the same time, however, individual challenges in product development can also find a place here. International networks can provide new perspectives on one's own issues. In addition, they provide easy access to current developments at the international level, e.g., with regard to current developments within the EU. A concrete and good possibility to find new partners and networks and, therefore, also new knowledge is the participation in scientific projects on the topic of nature-based and health-promoting tourism. These projects can be anchored regionally, nationally, or internationally.

3 Conclusion

The KPI approach supports regional tourism development that focuses on the use and protection of natural resources and the health of guests. At the same time, however, numerous other aspects of the overall development are also considered, thus promoting a development that is aligned with the principles of sustainability.

As with the idea of sustainability, the KPI approach is implemented from a view of the big picture to a detailed consideration of the regional situation, considering supra-regional trends and framework conditions. In this way, different development paths for a very concrete development of offers in the region can be identified and assessed.

However, the actual implementation in a region is also associated with potential obstacles. Thus, the KPI approach is initially embedded in an overall process that additionally requires both upstream and downstream activities. These, in turn, are associated with the use of financial and time resources. Moreover, this form of development is not feasible for most regions on their own, as medical expertise is required in addition to tourism expertise. This becomes particularly clear when the aim is to develop a region's own evidence, tailored to its natural resources. Possible solutions are to be seen in the cooperations of several partners as well as in a (co-)financing of the project via public funding, e.g., in the form of practice-oriented research projects, as the EU supports them through the Interreg programs.

Within the KPI approach, it must also be considered that the optimal conditions used for the analysis must be regularly reviewed and adjusted, not least in view of the available evidence. This also applies to the consideration of future tourism trends. A transfer of the approach to regions outside the Alps, which is possible in principle, also requires an adjustment of the indicators to the respective (natural) conditions.

Overall, there is still a need for further development. This is not necessarily limited to tourism development but can also be extended to other areas against the background of the described references to sustainability. One example is certainly the use of nature-based offers with medical evidence in the context of prevention, therapy, or rehabilitation measures in the sense of a holistic public health strategy.

References

1. W. Bätzing, *Zwischen Wildnis und Freizeitpark: eine Streitschrift zur Zukunft der Alpen* (Rotpunktverlag, Zürich, 2015)
2. W. Bätzing, Der Alpentourismus: Verdrängungswettbewerb der Großen oder dezentrales Potenzial für Alpentäler? (2019)
3. C.L. Correa-Martínez, S. Kampmeier, P. Kümpers, V. Schwierzeck, M. Hennies, W. Hafezi, J. Kühn, H. Pavenstädt, S. Ludwig, A. Mellmann, A pandemic in times of global tourism: superspreading and exportation of COVID-19 cases from a ski area in Austria. J. Clin. Microbiol. **58**, e00588-e620 (2020). https://doi.org/10.1128/JCM.00588-20
4. S. Gössling, D. Scott, C.M. Hall, Pandemics, tourism and global change: a rapid assessment of COVID-19. J. Sustain. Tour. **29**, 1–20 (2021). https://doi.org/10.1080/09669582.2020.1758708
5. A.M. Lenart-Boroń, P.M. Boroń, J.A. Prajsnar, M.W. Guzik, M.S. Żelazny, M.D. Pufelska, M.J. Chmiel, COVID-19 lockdown shows how much natural mountain regions are affected by heavy tourism. Sci. Total Environ. **806**, 151355 (2022). https://doi.org/10.1016/j.scitotenv.2021.151355
6. E. Heymann, E. Heymann, Coronavirus: a threat to the business of traditional tourist destinations. 3

7. DIHK—Deutscher Industrie- und Handelskammertag: DIHK-Report Fachkräfte 2021. https://www.dihk.de/resource/blob/61638/9bde58258a88d4fce8cda7e2ef300b9c/dihk-report-fachkraeftesicherung-2021-data.pdf. (2021)
8. Statistik Austria: Ankünfte, Nächtigungen im Tourismus 2021: Knapp ein Fünftel weniger Nächtigungen als 2020. https://www.statistik.at/web_de/statistiken/wirtschaft/tourismus/beherbergung/ankuenfte_naechtigungen/index.html. Accessed 2022/03/28
9. BMU—Bundesministerium für Umwelt, Naturschutz und Reaktorsicherheit: Alpenkonvention konkret: Ziele und Umsetzung. https://www.alpconv.org/fileadmin/user_upload/Publications/AS/AS2_DE.pdf. (2004)
10. European Commission: EU strategy for sustainable tourism. https://www.europarl.europa.eu/doceo/document/TA-9-2021-0109_EN.html. (2021)
11. Alpenkonvention: Nachhaltiger Tourismus in Den Alpen—Alpenzustandsbericht. https://www.alpconv.org/fileadmin/user_upload/Publications/RSA/RSA4_DE.pdf. (2013).
12. M. Shakya, Nachhaltigkeit im Tourismus—Anspruch, Wirklichkeit und Umsetzungsmöglichkeiten. in *Nachhaltiger Konsum*, , ed by W. Wellbrock, D. Ludin(Springer Fachmedien Wiesbaden, Wiesbaden 2021), pp. 853–870. https://doi.org/10.1007/978-3-658-33353-9_51
13. World Tourism Organization (UNWTO), European Travel Commission (ETC) eds: Exploring Health Tourism—Executive Summary. World Tourism Organization (UNWTO) (2018). https://doi.org/10.18111/9789284420308
14. V. Boschetto Doorly, *Megatrends defining the future of tourism: A Journey Within the Journey in 12 Universal Truths* (Springer International Publishing, Cham 2020). https://doi.org/10.1007/978-3-030-48626-6
15. Zukunftsinstitut: Megatrend Gesundheit. https://www.zukunftsinstitut.de/dossier/megatrend-gesundheit/. Accessed 2022/03/29
16. R. de Macedo Couto, D.F. Brandespim, A review of the one health concept and its application as a tool for policy-makers. Int. J. One Health **6**, 83–89 (2020). https://doi.org/10.14202/IJOH.2020.83-89
17. A. Hartl, C. Geyer, Heilkraft der Alpen. Benevento, Elsbethen (2020)
18. E. Pessot, D. Spoladore, A. Zangiacomi, M. Sacco, Natural resources in health tourism: a systematic literature review. Sustainability **13**, 2661 (2021). https://doi.org/10.3390/su13052661
19. C. Pichler, A. Hartl, Die alpine Gesundheitsregion SalzburgerLand. Evidenzbasierter Gesundheitstourismus als Chance für den Alpenraum. in: Alpenreisen: Erlebnis, Raumtransformationen, Imagination. pp. 421–444. StudienVerlag, Innsbruck Wien Bozen (2017)
20. G.C. Steckenbauer, S. Tischler, A. Hartl, C. Pichler, Destination and product development rested on evidence-based health tourism. in *The Routledge Handbook of Health Tourism*, ed. by M.K. Smith, L. Puczkó (Routledge, Taylor & Francis Group, New York 2017), pp. 315–331
21. PWC—PriceWaterhouseCoopers: Ein neues Gesundheitsbewusstsein für Deutschland. https://www.pwc.de/de/gesundheitswesen-und-pharma/ein-neues-gesundheitsbewusstsein-fuer-deutschland.pdf. (2021)
22. B.X. Lee, F. Kjaerulf, S. Turner, L. Cohen, P.D. Donnelly, R. Muggah, R. Davis, A. Realini, B. Kieselbach, L.S. MacGregor, I. Waller, R. Gordon, M. Moloney-Kitts, G. Lee, J. Gilligan, Transforming our world: implementing the 2030 agenda through sustainable development goal indicators. J. Public Health Pol. **37**, 13–31 (2016). https://doi.org/10.1057/s41271-016-0002-7
23. D. Spoladore, E. Pessot, M. Bischof, A. Hartl, M. Sacco, Collaborative design approach for the development of an ontology-based decision support system in health tourism. in *Smart and Sustainable Collaborative Networks 4.0,* ed. by L.M. Camarinha-Matos, X. Boucher, H. Afsarmanesh (Springer International Publishing, Cham 2021), pp. 632–639. https://doi.org/10.1007/978-3-030-85969-5_59
24. D. Spoladore, E. Pessot, An ontology-based decision support system to foster innovation and competitiveness opportunities of health tourism destinations. in *Digital and Strategic Innovation for Alpine Health Tourism - Natural Resources, Digital Tools and Innovation Practices from HEALPS 2 Project*, ed. by D. Spoladore, E. Pessot, M. Sacco. (2022)

25. C. Pichler, A. Hartl, R. Weißböck-Erdheim, M. Bischof, Medical evidence of Alpine natural resources as a base for health tourism. in *Digital and Strategic Innovation for Alpine Health Tourism—Natural Resources, Digital Tools and Innovation Practices from HEALPS 2 Project*, ed. by D. Spoladore, E. Pessot, M. Saccpo (2022)
26. P. de Paula, J. Niebauer, Effects of high altitude training on exercise capacity: fact or myth. Sleep Breath. **16**, 233–239 (2012). https://doi.org/10.1007/s11325-010-0445-1
27. von Mutius, E., Vercelli, D.: Farm living: effects on childhood asthma and allergy. Nat. Rev. Immunol. 10, 861–868 (2010). https://doi.org/10.1038/nri2871
28. J. Kaiser, Immunology. How farm life prevents asthma. Science. **349**, 1034 (2015). https://doi.org/10.1126/science.349.6252.1034
29. J. Prossegger, D. Huber, C. Grafetstätter, C. Pichler, R. Weisböck-Erdheim, B. Iglseder, G. Wewerka, A. Hartl, Effects of moderate mountain hiking and balneotherapy on community-dwelling older people: a randomized controlled trial. Exp. Gerontol. **122**, 74–84 (2019). https://doi.org/10.1016/j.exger.2019.04.006
30. J. Schmude, P.Namberger, Tourismusgeographie. WBG (Wissenschaftliche Buchgesellschaft), Darmstadt (2015)
31. E.J. Jordan, L. Lesar, D.M. Spencer, Clarifying the interrelations of residents' perceived tourism-related stress, stressors, and impacts. J. Travel Res. **60**, 208–219 (2021). https://doi.org/10.1177/0047287519888287
32. F. Martínez-Roget, X.A. Rodríguez, Academic Tourism: Conceptual and Theoretical Issues. in *Academic Tourism*, ed. by J.P. Cerdeira Bento, F. Martínez-Roget, E.T. Pereira, X.A. Rodríguez. (Springer International Publishing, Cham 2021), pp. 7–20. https://doi.org/10.1007/978-3-030-57288-4_2
33. R. Butler, Seasonality in tourism: Issues and implications. Tourist Rev **53**, 18–24 (1998). https://doi.org/10.1108/eb058278
34. W.C. Terry, Solving seasonality in tourism? labour shortages and guest worker programmes in the USA: solving seasonality in tourism? Area **48**, 111–118 (2016). https://doi.org/10.1111/area.12242
35. U. Hapke, Psychische Gesundheit in der Bevölkerung. Aktuelle Daten und Hintergründe. Robert Koch Institut (2015)
36. RKI—Robert-Koch-Institut: Journal of Health Monitoring—Prävalenz von Rücken- und Nackenschmerzen in Deutschland. Ergebnisse der Krankheitslast-Studie BURDEN 2020. https://www.rki.de/DE/Content/Gesundheitsmonitoring/Gesundheitsberichterstattung/GBEDownloadsJ/JoHM_S3_2021_Rueckenschmerz_Nackenschmerz.pdf. (2021)
37. M. Karl, C. Reintinger, Mapping destination choice: set theory as a methodological tool. in *Tourist behaviour: an international perspective*, ed. by M. Kozak, N. Kozak (CABI, Wallingford 2016), pp. 74–83. https://doi.org/10.1079/9781780648125.0074
38. T.W. Leigh, The consumer quest for authenticity: the multiplicity of meanings within the mg subculture of consumption. J. Acad. Mark. Sci. **34**, 481–493 (2006). https://doi.org/10.1177/0092070306288403
39. S. Heitmann, Authenticity in tourism. in *Research themes for tourism*, ed. by P. Robinson, S. Heitmann, P. Dieke (CABI, Wallingford 2011), pp. 45–58. https://doi.org/10.1079/9781845936846.0045
40. G. Tiberghien, H. Bremner, S. Milne, Authenticity and disorientation in the tourism experience. J. Outdoor Recreat. Tour. **30**, 100283 (2020). https://doi.org/10.1016/j.jort.2020.100283
41. P. Beritelli, Cooperation among prominent actors in a tourist destination. Ann. Tour. Res. **38**, 607–629 (2011). https://doi.org/10.1016/j.annals.2010.11.015
42. J. Elliott, Tourism: politics and public sector management. Routledge (2020). https://doi.org/10.4324/9781003070986
43. Y.-F. Leung, A. Spenceley, G. Hvenegaard, R. Buckley (ed.), *Tourism and visitor management in protected areas : guidelines for sustainability*. IUCN, International Union for Conservation of Nature (2018). https://doi.org/10.2305/IUCN.CH.2018.PAG.27.en
44. G.I. Novolodskaya, T.Y. Kramarova, K.A. Lebedev, L.A. Ponkratova, E.Y. Chicherova, Public-private partnership as innovative form of attraction of financial resources in sphere of tourism. J. Environ. Manag. Tour. **9**, 714 (2018). https://doi.org/10.14505//jemt.v9.4(28).04

Open Access This chapter is licensed under the terms of the Creative Commons Attribution 4.0 International License (http://creativecommons.org/licenses/by/4.0/), which permits use, sharing, adaptation, distribution and reproduction in any medium or format, as long as you give appropriate credit to the original author(s) and the source, provide a link to the Creative Commons license and indicate if changes were made.

The images or other third party material in this chapter are included in the chapter's Creative Commons license, unless indicated otherwise in a credit line to the material. If material is not included in the chapter's Creative Commons license and your intended use is not permitted by statutory regulation or exceeds the permitted use, you will need to obtain permission directly from the copyright holder.

Alpine Assets, Perceptions and Strategies for Nature-Based Health Tourism

Jan Mosedale, Arnulf Hartl, Christina Pichler, and Michael Bischof

Abstract Nature-based health tourism is experiencing a resurgence. To determine its potential as a development opportunity for alpine destinations, it is necessary to analyse both the demand and supply side. Two surveys were conducted: a representative survey of the population of six countries of the Alpine Space exploring the perception of the Alps as a healthy destination in general and on the personal assessment of the health effect of natural resources in particular and an exploratory survey of tourism stakeholders in destination management, accommodation and gastronomy as well as (health) tourism services with a focus on the expected economic developments and the relevance of individual target groups for nature-based health tourism. The results demonstrate the need for a strategic development process which aligns perceptions with destination strategy and pre-existing offers. Two potential strategies are briefly outlined: 1. destinations with non-locally specific alpine natural health resources can develop broad tourism experiences for health conditions that occur across society with health a secondary aspect in marketing. 2. destinations featuring locally specific natural health resources with proven evidence can develop offers for a specific condition and are thus able to target a very specific group.

Keywords Nature-based health tourism · Natural health resources · Supply · Demand · Perceptions

1 Introduction

Nature-based health tourism was particularly popular in the nineteenth century and is therefore not a new phenomenon. Yet, the popularity of this type of health tourism had faded over time due to the increasing quality of medical interventions and changes to

J. Mosedale (✉)
Institute for Tourism and Leisure, University of Applied Sciences of the Grisons, Chur, Switzerland
e-mail: jan.mosedale@fhgr.ch

A. Hartl · C. Pichler · M. Bischof
Institute of Ecomedicine, Paracelsus Medical Private University, Salzburg, Austria

the structure of the health sector. Despite these changes, some destinations (particularly those with extensive infrastructure) have continued to offer nature-based health tourism products albeit often in combination with other tourism products. Based on recent research on the health benefits provided by nature in general and certain natural resources in specific [1] have led some individual tourism service providers and tourism to develop innovative evidence-based tourism experiences based on the health benefits of nature.

Trend forecasts have long predicted an increasing likelihood of Europeans viewing nature as an idyllic place for relaxation and withdrawal [2]. In particular, nature is valued highly as a source of peace of mind, strength, and integrity [3]. In a study examining the recommendations of Swedish inhabitants in urban areas to a friend who is feeling stressed, the respondents' first choice was to recommend a walk in the forest [4]. This subjective perception of the beneficial effects of nature is confirmed by empirical research analysing exposure to nature (either walking 15 min in a natural setting or watching videos of a natural setting), which leads to positive emotions and increases human reflection capacities and the ability to complete attentional tasks [5]. While exercising in nature also provides long-term health benefits [6].

With its tools and practices [7], the HEALPS2 project provides an innovative framework for the (further) development of such health-promoting tourism offers. In order to better adapt these offerings to the needs of the market, it makes sense to take a closer look at demand and supply. On the demand side of nature-based health tourism, this includes the perceptions of nature-based health tourism in general, the perceptions of the Alps as a landscape with health benefits, and the types of diseases and health restrictions that respondents can see themselves address via nature-based health tourism. The level of interest, needs, and expectations of tourists regarding the health benefits of environmental resources in the Alpine region provides a basis for assessing the feasibility of nature-based health tourism offers.

On the supply side, a first necessary step is an analysis of the situation regarding nature-based health tourism [8]. In addition to existing natural health resources, representing the core of the tourism experience, services and socio-cultural offers in the destination should also be analyzed for this purpose. A key success factor for the development of nature-based health tourism is the cooperation of the various stakeholders on the supply side (particularly across the tourism and medical sectors) [9]. The potential on the supply-side must be matched with the needs and expectations of the guests, on the one hand, and with the expected market potential, on the other hand. Although there is an increasing demand for nature-based and health-promoting services and the possibility to differentiate the destination portfolio of tourism experiences based on this form of tourism, the market segment is still relatively small. Thus, despite the fundamentally high quality of supply and the achievable prices, this market segment is only suitable in a few cases as a supporting pillar of the tourism economy for entire regions. As a complimentary tourism experience, nature-based health offers should be compatible with the basic strategy and orientation of the tourism services in the destination. For example, the destination image should fit this type of tourism as well as the existing attractions in the destination or the currently strongest target segment. The consideration of the current and future target segments is certainly an essential part of the supply-side analysis.

All in all, the development of nature-based health tourism is a medium- to long-term development perspective that requires an in-depth analysis of both the demand and the supply side to increase the economic potential of the Alpine region.

2 Methods

A representative survey [10] of the demand side covering six countries of the Alpine Space (Austria, France, Germany, Italy, Slovenia, and Switzerland) was completed with a sample size of $n = 3{,}334$ individuals. The data are representative of age, gender, and education and were first analyzed for correlated indications using a factor analysis. 18 indications were deleted from further analysis, and seven indications remained: allergies, stress & burnout, back pain, lack of fitness, overweight, and respiratory and cardiovascular conditions. The survey included questions on the perception of the Alps as a healthy destination in general and on the personal assessment of the health effect of natural resources in particular. In addition, questions were asked about personal health, booking behaviour for nature-based health tourism, and the importance of services for such a holiday.

On the supply side, an explorative online survey [10] was conducted in the German Alps, in which a total of 73 stakeholders from the fields of destination management, accommodation, and gastronomy, as well as (health) tourism services, participated. In this context, the expected economic developments in the field of nature-based health tourism as well as the relevance of individual target groups for such types of offers in a time horizon until 2030 were analysed.

In the following, the results and graphics for both described evaluations can be found.

3 Results

3.1 Perceptions of Alpine Natural Resources in the Context of Health

The evidence base for natural health resources is not common knowledge. Therefore, the perceptions of nature-based health tourism in general, natural landscapes, and particular natural resources are key for understanding the potential of nature-based health tourism. This perception is even more important as the perception of natural landscapes, and natural health resources may affect the health benefits derived from a nature-based health tourism holiday [11].

The results of the survey show that 86.7% of the survey respondents perceive natural environments as providing health benefits (see Table 1). The perception that natural environments provide health benefits is a key basis for the development of nature-based health tourism products, yet, in comparison, fewer of the respondents (50.1%) take possible health benefits into account when choosing their holiday destination. This discrepancy could have three reasons: first, that health benefits are not usually the main reason for travelling; second, that respondents do not equate health with relaxation; and third, that they have too little information regarding health benefits to be able to consider these when planning a holiday. Regardless, 61.3% of respondents state that I pay attention to my health when on holiday.

Due to its diversity of natural resources with health benefits, the Alpine region offers a high potential for the development of health tourism products (see Chap. 1). This is mirrored by the perception of 78.5% of respondents that the Alps are a good health tourism destination.

Health treatments based on scientific evidence are vital for ensuring the accreditation of Alpine health tourism products by health insurance companies [12]. However, lay persons are not in a position to know the scientific evidence of health benefits of natural resources. Figure 1 shows, on the one hand, the perception of the respondents of health benefits of a given alpine natural resource in the treatment of back pain and, on the other hand, the level of scientific evidence for each resource on a range from 1 (low evidence) to 10 (high evidence). Not surprisingly, a comparison of the perception with the evidence reveals a certain lack of scientific knowledge of the respondents. The natural resources "Radon treatment" and "health caves", for instance have a

Table 1 Perceptions of nature-based health tourism

	Strongly agree (%)	Agree (%)	Neither agree nor disagree (%)	Disagree (%)	Strongly disagree (%)
Natural environments provide health benefits	42	44.7	13.3	3.5	1.3
I take possible health benefits into account when deciding where to go on holiday	15.0	35.1	31.9	12.7	5.3
I pay attention to my health when on holiday	17.9	43.4	26.6	9.2	2.8
The Alps are a good health tourism destination	31.6	46.9	16.3	3.4	1.9

high level of scientific evidence, but their health benefits are not perceived by the respondents as being particularly high. In contrast, the health benefits of "Forests" are perceived as being high but do not have such a high scientific evidence level. The evidence of health benefits achieved via natural resources needs to be at the centre of product development and subsequent marketing for health tourists to be able to distinguish nature-based health tourism from wellness.

Another important factor important for marketing nature-based health tourism are the different diseases or potential health restrictions that potential guests are interested in treating or in taking preventative measures during a nature-based health holiday (see Fig. 2). With 64% back pain is the main disease/restriction that respondents of the survey are interested in addressing, followed by diseases/restrictions that consist of a combination of physical and mental factors. Of particular interest are the perceptions of the target group of possible treatment/prevention measures. Figure 3 shows these perceptions for the target group "back pain" in combination with the evidence level of the particular treatment/prevention measure. Similar to the perceptions of and evidence for natural resources (see Fig. 1), the results demonstrate a certain discrepancy between the perception of the impact of treatment/prevention and its evidence level for some treatments/types of prevention, with some being underestimated (e.g., yoga and climbing), while the effectiveness of other treatments/types of prevention is overestimated (e.g., nutritional advice and cosmetics/beauty offer).

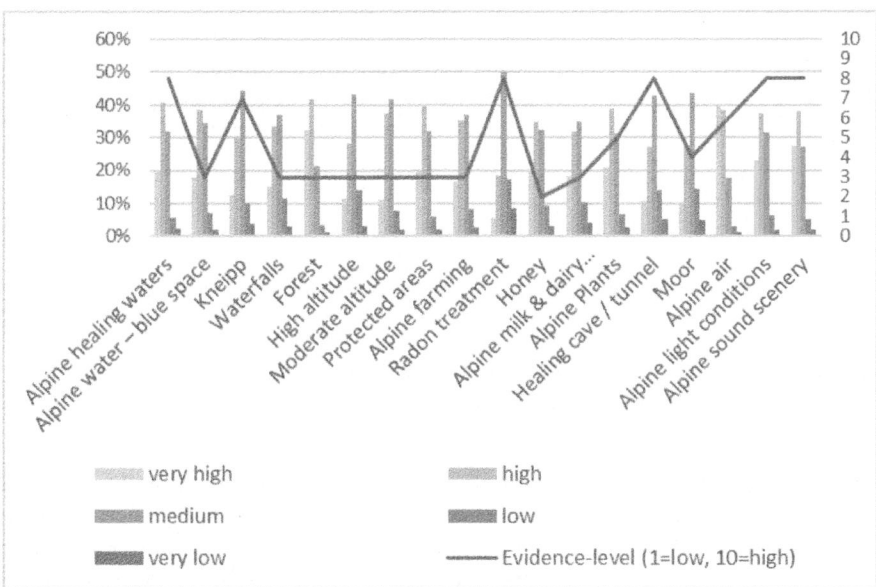

Fig. 1 Assessment of health benefits of natural resources from the perspective of guests with back pain and current level of evidence for these resources

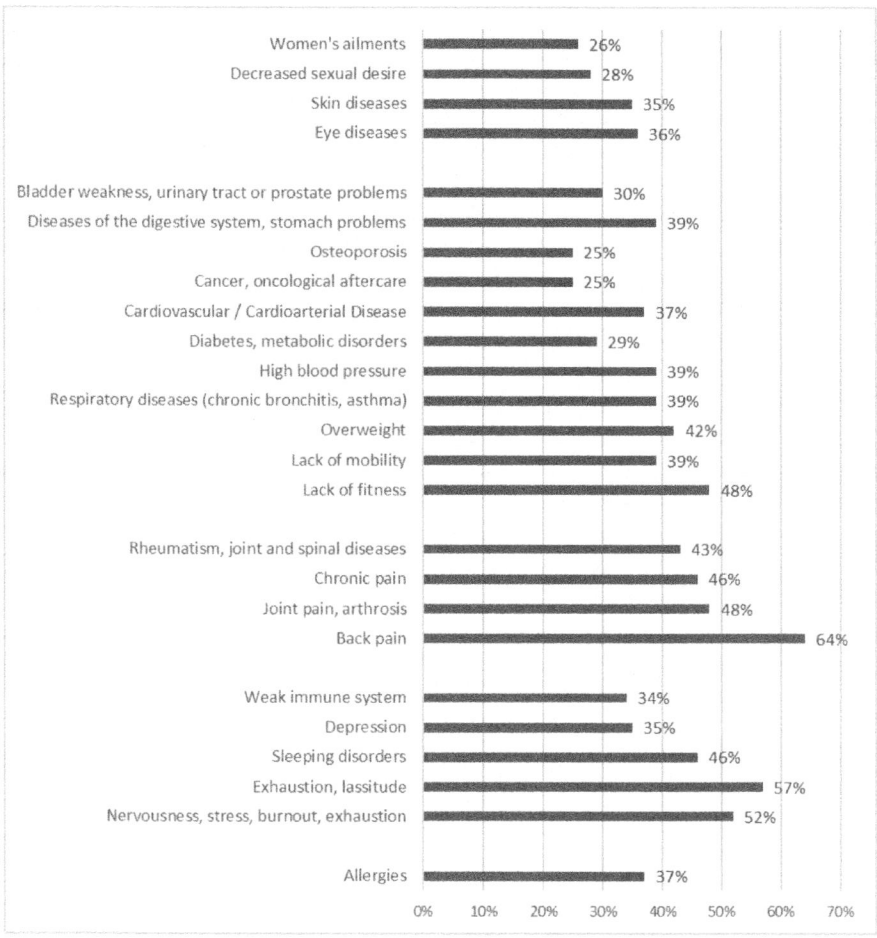

Fig. 2 Interest in treatment and correlation of health conditions from the guests' perspective

3.2 Supply-Side Strategies for and Perspectives on Nature-Based Health Tourism

On the supply side, there are an increasing number of examples of the implementation of nature-based health tourism products [13]. Due to the necessary expertise in the fields of tourism and medicine, there is nevertheless still a great need for knowledge transfer into practice. This is especially true for medical knowledge about the cause-and-effect relationships between natural resources and human health.

The results of the survey show that it is also worthwhile to address the issue of nature-based health tourism from a supply-side perspective. The service providers were asked to assess the economic success of existing nature-based health tourism services and to estimate its development up to the year 2030 (see Fig. 4). Today,

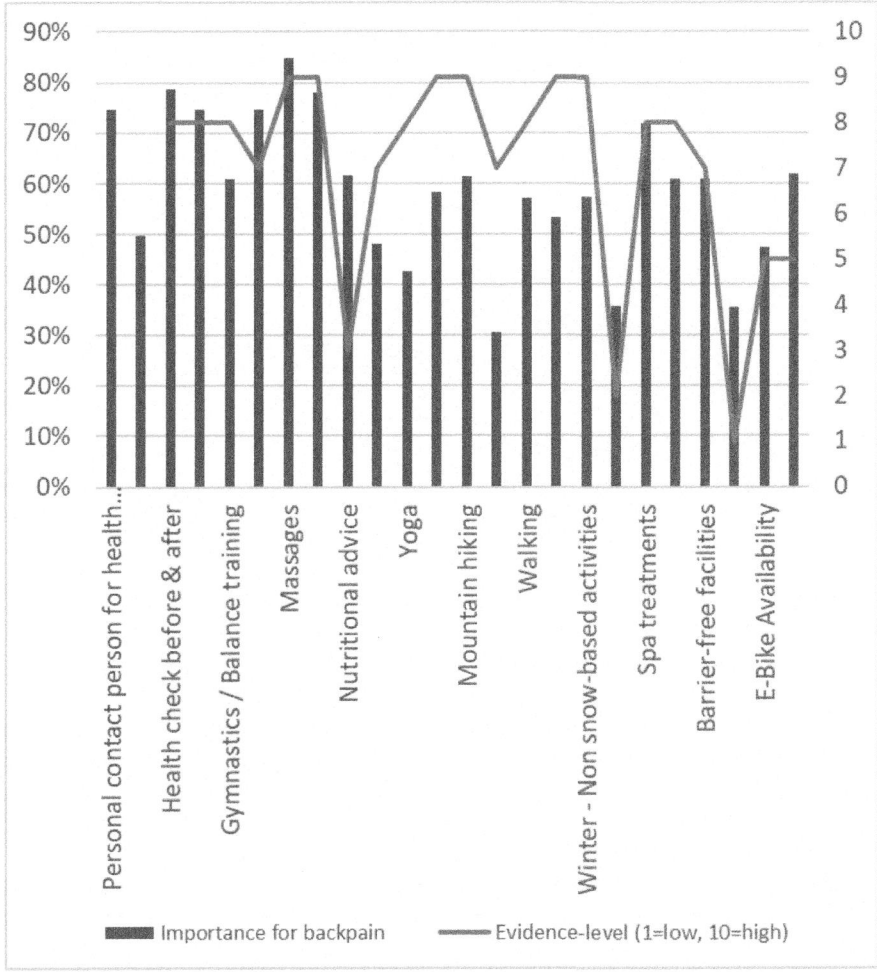

Fig. 3 Importance of booking factors for a nature-based health holiday from the perspective of guests with back pain and current level of evidence for these factors

these offers already contribute above-average to the success of the service providers. Thus, 57.2% of respondents state that these services currently range from "good" to "very good" success.

In perspective up to 2030, this value rises to 76.2%. In this respect, this type of tourism not only has great potential from a scientific and thus rather theoretical point of view but also seems to be a worthwhile development path for the practical actors.

If the above-mentioned relationships between natural resources and health effects are well-defined and there is an overview of the own service portfolio as well as the natural features, the focus should be on the selection of suitable target groups. The target groups can be differentiated according to various characteristics. To develop

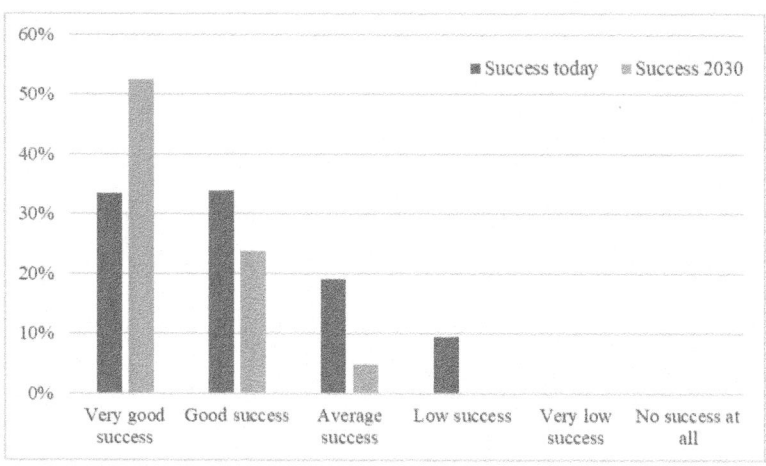

Fig. 4 Economic success of offers in nature-based health tourism today and expectations for 2030 from the perspective of the supplier side

suitable offers, it is particularly important to consider the health-related motivation and the composition of the tourists, e.g., individuals or families. A first analysis of the importance of the target group constellation from the providers' point of view, it becomes apparent that primarily couples and individuals are of interest for nature-based health tourism offers (see Fig. 5). Accordingly, these two target groups need to be addressed more intensively in the future. More than 65% of respondents want to increase their focus on couples, and almost 40% on individuals. Families (12% increased targeting) or other groups (3.5% increased targeting) play a rather subordinate role from the providers' point of view.

As demonstrated for the demand side, the various diseases or possible health restrictions that potential guests are interested in treating or preventing during a nature-based health holiday are an important factor for the development of offers. Conversely, the suppliers' assessment of the current and future importance of the various health-related target groups is also of interest in this context (see Fig. 6). The results of the survey initially show similar values for both maintaining health or building physical resilience and maintaining health or building mental resilience. Around 57% of respondents currently rate both target groups (physical and mental health) as very or absolutely important. In the expectation of future developments, these values rise to more than 70% in the case of physical health and to around 75% in the case of mental health. If this question is examined in more detail, it becomes apparent that, from the providers' point of view, guests suffering from psychological stress are an important target group for nature-based health tourism. Currently, about 69% of the providers state that these guests are very or absolutely important for their own offer. In the future, the providers also expect a rise in importance here. Thus, approx. 83% of the respondents state that these guests will be very to absolutely important in the future. Guests with physical complaints (e.g., orthopedic conditions

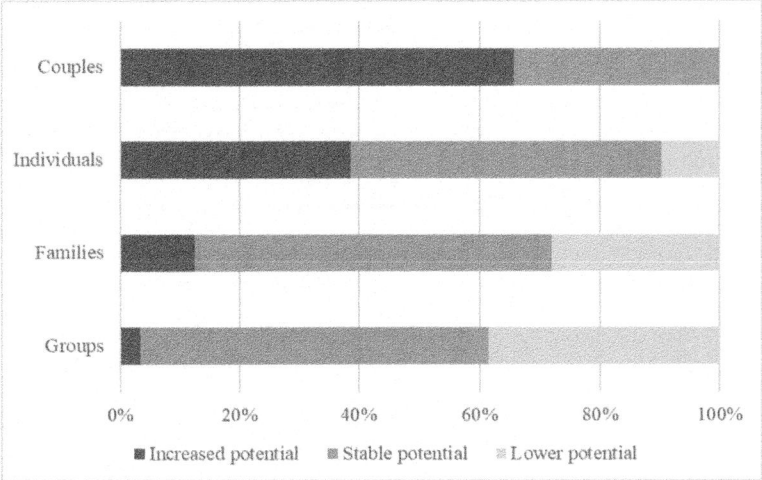

Fig. 5 Potential target groups for nature-based health tourism in the future from the perspective of tourism service providers

such as back pain or cardiovascular conditions) also play an important role, but these target groups play such an important role for fewer providers, both currently and in future expectations. The values for these two target groups are currently 48% (orthopedic conditions very to absolutely important) and 56% (cardiovascular conditions very to absolutely important), respectively, and increase to nearly 72% (orthopedic conditions very to absolutely important) and nearly 69% (cardiovascular conditions very to absolutely important), respectively, in providers' future expectations. In this respect, the expected increase in the importance of guests with orthopedic conditions is particularly high. Finally, the providers were asked in this context about the importance of guests who have health problems due to urban and fine dust diseases as a motive. Here, the lowest values for the surveyed motives are found, both currently (41% very to absolutely important) and in the future (66% very to absolutely important).

4 Discussion

Each destination will possess a different set of natural health resources suitable for various health conditions with diverse levels of evidence. At the same time, most regions considering developing nature-based health tourism will already have some tourism development. Therefore, the strategic development of nature-based health tourism requires the consideration of both supply and demand in a strategic process adapted to the specific situation in the destination to ensure that the nature-based health tourism offers are in alignment with destination strategy and pre-existing offers.

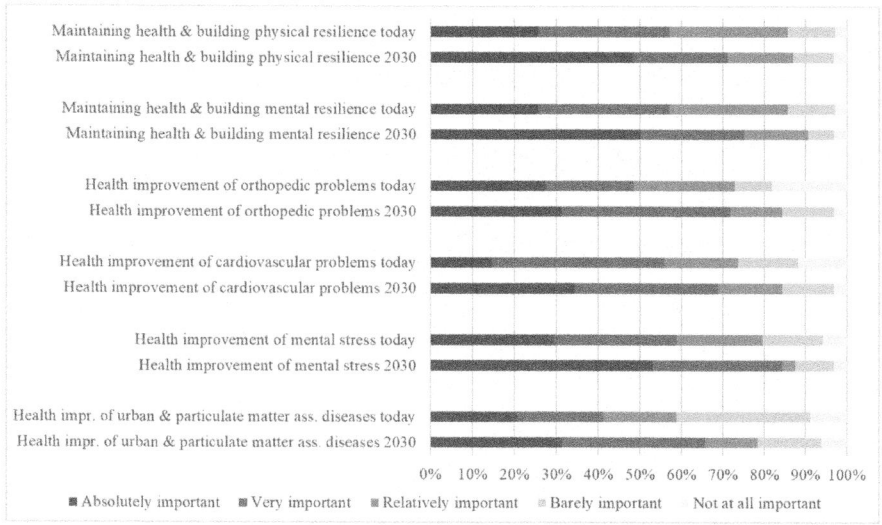

Fig. 6 Importance of health-related target groups for today and future supply in 2030

Destinations that feature locally specific natural health resources with proven evidence can develop offers for a specific condition and are thus able to target a very specific group. While this locally specific nature-based health tourism will only cater to a niche market, it can provide a unique selling proposition that cannot be copied by other destinations and can serve to diversify the tourism product, e.g., by extending the season or offering a product in the low season. In addition, these nature-based health tourism services may increase the added value in the region, as several service providers collaborate across sectors (most prominently tourism and the medical sector). However, as the marketing of this type of locally specific natural resource is entirely focused on the health benefits of the natural resource, it is particularly important that there is a high level of evidence for these health benefits. Local clinical studies may be undertaken to underline the health benefits of these resources and should feature prominently in the marketing.

While destinations with non-locally specific alpine natural health resources can develop broad tourism experiences for health conditions that occur across society. In this case, the health tourism aspect of the experience does not need to be at the core of marketing activities but should be incorporated within the experience and the marketing as an additional advantage of a "regular" holiday. On the one hand, such a marketing strategy caters to those tourism service providers who see illness as a stigma and do not want to associate their services with such a stigma. In addition, as demonstrated by the results of the survey of the alpine population, the general perception of the health benefits of some natural resources (e.g., alpine air and forests) are not supported by scientific evidence. Despite this lack of scientific evidence, these natural resources should feature in the general marketing materials (of course, without a direct attribution to potential health benefits).

5 Conclusions

This chapter highlights that there is a demand for nature-based health tourism. Tourism service providers (at least in the case study analysed) see the potential of this type of tourism development. Yet the potential of nature-based health tourism can be further extended by including prevention as an important factor in ensuring and increasing public health. However, the public health care system is currently dominated by a paradigm focused on medical intervention. A shift in public health policy and related funding structures (e.g., health insurance) towards nature-based prevention and treatment will only occur if the health benefits of natural health resources can be monetized as ecosystem services [14] and compared with the costs of classical medicine. Academic research measuring the financial contributions of natural health resources and the savings accrued by public health institutions is necessary to determine the overall potential of nature-based health tourism in the future.

References

1. C. Pichler, A. Hartl, R. Weißböck-Erdheim, M. Bischof, Medical evidence of Alpine natural resources as a base for health tourism. in *Digital and Strategic Innovation for Alpine Health Tourism—Natural Resources, Digital Tools and Innovation Practices from HEALPS 2 Project*, ed. by D. Spoladore, E. Pessot, M. Sacco (2022)
2. N. Lüdi, K. Frick, D. Bosshart, S. Kaiser, M. Hauser, M. Kühne, A. Egli, E. Banz, Unabhängige Studie des Gottlieb Duttweiler Instituts im Auftrag von Pro Natura. 68
3. Trendbüro and Kantar: Zukunftsstudie Living 2038, (2017)
4. P. Grahn, U.A. Stigsdotter, Landscape planning and stress. Urban For. Urban Greening. **2**, 1–18 (2003). https://doi.org/10.1078/1618-8667-00019
5. F.S. Mayer, C.M. Frantz, E. Bruehlman-Senecal, K. Dolliver, Why is nature beneficial?: the role of connectedness to nature. Environ. Behav. **41**, 607–643 (2009). https://doi.org/10.1177/0013916508319745
6. J. Barton, J. Pretty, What is the best dose of nature and green exercise for improving mental health? A Multi-Study Anal. Environ. Sci. Technol. **44**, 3947–3955 (2010). https://doi.org/10.1021/es903183r
7. M. Bischof, A. Hartl, KPI for data-driven assessment of innovative development paths for nature-based health tourism in the Alpine region. in *Digital and Strategic Innovation for Alpine Health Tourism—Natural Resources, Digital Tools and Innovation Practices from HEALPS 2 Project*, ed. by D. Spoladore, E. Pessot, M. Sacco (2022)
8. C. McLennan, L. Ruhanen, B. Ritchie, T. Pham, Dynamics of destination development: investigating the application of transformation theory. J. Hospitality Tourism Res. **36**, 164–190 (2012). https://doi.org/10.1177/1096348010390816
9. H. Ness, J. Aarstad, S.A. Haugland, B.O. Grønseth, Destination development: the role of interdestination bridge ties. J. Travel Res. **53**, 183–195 (2014). https://doi.org/10.1177/0047287513491332
10. L. Gideon (ed.), *Handbook of survey methodology for the social sciences* (Springer, New York, 2012)
11. L. Menatti, A. Casado da Rocha, Landscape and health: connecting psychology, aesthetics, and philosophy through the concept of affordance. Front. Psychol. **7**, (2016). https://doi.org/10.3389/fpsyg.2016.00571

12. A. Hartl, C. Pichler, R. Lymann, G.C. Steckenbauer, Gesundheitstourismus in den Alpen. Natur als Basis wirksamer Anwendungen. in *Schweizer Jahrbuch für Tourismus: Gesellschaftlicher Wandel als Herausforderung im alpinen Tourismus* T. Bieger, P. Beritelli, C. Laesser. (Erich Schmidt Verlag, Berlin 2016)
13. M.S. Groß, *Gesundheitstourismus* (UVK Verlagsgesellschaft mbH mit UVK/Lucius, Konstanz München, 2017)
14. J. Farley, Ecosystem services: The economics debate. Ecosyt. Serv. **1**, 40–49 (2012). https://doi.org/10.1016/j.ecoser.2012.07.002

Open Access This chapter is licensed under the terms of the Creative Commons Attribution 4.0 International License (http://creativecommons.org/licenses/by/4.0/), which permits use, sharing, adaptation, distribution and reproduction in any medium or format, as long as you give appropriate credit to the original author(s) and the source, provide a link to the Creative Commons license and indicate if changes were made.

The images or other third party material in this chapter are included in the chapter's Creative Commons license, unless indicated otherwise in a credit line to the material. If material is not included in the chapter's Creative Commons license and your intended use is not permitted by statutory regulation or exceeds the permitted use, you will need to obtain permission directly from the copyright holder.

An Ontology-Based Decision Support System to Foster Innovation and Competitiveness Opportunities of Health Tourism Destinations

Daniele Spoladore and Elena Pessot

Abstract The competitiveness of nature-based Health Tourism (NHT) industry, especially in the Alpine regions, is increasingly linked to the sustainability and exploitation of unique natural resources of tourism destinations, which often lack the access to knowledge and networks of stakeholders to improve their offerings. In this sense, the use of digital tools can open up further opportunities to reconsider value offerings and better access different knowledge resources and relationships within the industry network. This Chapter illustrates the collaborative design approach adopted in HEALPS2 for the development of an ontology-based Decision Support System for health tourism destinations. The resulting ontology aims to model the relationships between the available natural resources, the value offerings and the target groups of NHT destinations. Moreover, the Collaborative Design approach foresees the involvement of end-users (i.e. not only tourism destinations, but also the network of stakeholders, and the actual and potential future tourists) as both sources of knowledge and validators of the ontology and its outputs, aiming to inform decision-making processes in a shared knowledge model that leverages on digital tools.

Keywords Health tourism · Evidence-based health tourism · Collaborative development · Ontology-based decision support system · Ontology · Alpine region

---

D. Spoladore (✉) · E. Pessot
Institute of Intelligent Industrial Technologies and Systems for Advanced Manufacturing (STIIMA) National Research Council of Italy, Lecco, Italy
e-mail: daniele.spoladore@stiima.cnr.it

E. Pessot
e-mail: elena.pessot@stiima.cnr.it

D. Spoladore
Department of Pure and Applied Sciences, Insubria University, Varese, Italy

© The Author(s) 2023
D. Spoladore et al. (eds.), *Digital and Strategic Innovation for Alpine Health Tourism*, SpringerBriefs in Applied Sciences and Technology,
https://doi.org/10.1007/978-3-031-15457-7_4

1 Introduction

Nature-based Health Tourism (NHT) sees tourists travelling with the goal of receiving healing treatments or enhancing specific health or mental through medically-proven offers based on the effects of natural resources on the human body [1, 2]. The competitiveness of NHT is strictly linked to the exploitation and sustainability of natural resources of tourism destinations: for example, natural healing resources as waterfalls, Alpine herbs and peculiar mountain microclimates offer proven health-promoting effects [3–5]. For the Alpine Space, natural resources play a pivotal role in NHT products, as they are peculiar unique selling propositions and leverage on the authenticity of the Alpine offerings [6]. The unique Alpine natural resources asset can potentially allow different local and regional stakeholders (e.g. tourism service providers, medical professionals, health providers, agriculture, crafts, etc.) to cooperate in the creation of new NHT value chains [2]. However, tourism destinations may lack the knowledge of relevant stakeholders involved in such activities, as well as the opportunity to actively access and participate in a NHT stakeholder network: as consequence, they could miss the opportunity to improve their capabilities in delivering offerings and exploiting the synergic combination of possible NHT sources and activities [7].

Hence, it emerges the need to identify, adopt and develop solutions able to facilitate the connection among regional and local key actors by exchanging evidence-based data and systematizing knowledge and local experiences. In this sense, different NHT stakeholders could greatly benefit from digital solutions, similarly to what is happening both in the healthcare and in the general tourism sectors—being revolutionized by digital tools such as the ones based on Artificial Intelligence and Semantic Web. This kind of digital solutions can foster cross-national cooperation, support the redefinition of competitiveness in the NHT services and deliver better management strategies [8].

This Chapter presents the engineering and development of a Decision Support System (DSS) based on the knowledge elicited from Alpine Space stakeholders of HEALPS2 project. This tool aims at serving as a shared knowledge-base to support Alpine health tourism stakeholders in further understanding the potentialities of their territory, and at suggesting services and natural resources to invest on [9, 10]. Specifically, the approach adopted to develop the HEALPS2 DSS strongly leverages on the sharing and capitalization of expertise and capabilities of the different stakeholders in a collaborative effort, considered fundamental for a successful adoption of digital solutions in the long term. The DSS developed in this section represents the base of the tool developed in Chap. 5 [11], where the ontology underlying the system is used to actively support destination managers and policy-makers.

The reminder of this Chapter is organized as follows: Sect. 2 highlights a few studies adopting ontologies in health or medical tourism contexts, while Sect. 3 underlines the opportunities of leveraging on an ontological approach. Section 4 delves into the ontology underlying the DSS, with focuses on the collaborative ontology engineering process adopted, on the deriving conceptualization and on the ontology's structure. Finally, the Conclusions summarize the main outcomes of this work.

2 Related Work

The adoption of ontologies and Semantic Web technologies for the development of DSSs in the tourism industry is widely documented in scientific literature. Moreover, shared and cooperative ontology engineering is also underlined as a success factor for such DSSs [12]. Nonetheless, there are very few examples of ontology-based DSSs specifically devoted to the industry of health tourism.

The ontological approach is the basis of the work of Chantrapornchai et al. [13], in which health tourism-related information are gathered and organized: domain experts' opinion is used as a way to evaluate the ontology's output. Two examples of ontology-based representations leverage on formalized knowledge to model touristic contexts [14] and provide user-dedicated recommendation in the field of medical tourism in Tunisia [15]. Lee et al. [16] proposed a smart orchestrator leveraging semantic models to formalize knowledge from the medical tourism, general tourism and medical treatment domains.

This work introduces an ontology-based DSS for the formal representation of health tourism destinations' natural resources, services provided and activities based on available natural resources. The ontology is developed leveraging on stakeholders' cooperation efforts and tourism data, with the aim of enhancing the value chain in a cooperative effort and in multiple rounds of knowledge exchange.

3 The Ontology-Based Approach

The HEALPS2 DSS leverages on Partners, stakeholders and destinations' knowledge to deliver suggestions on the economic and competitive potential of nature-based health tourism in the Alpine regions. Particularly, these regions are characterized by a variety of natural health resources and high environmental quality, but they are still not sufficiently integrated in value chains to properly face the demanding market of health travelers.

A promising approach to engineer a digital tool capable of making use of the knowledge shared among Alpine stakeholders is the ontology. Defined as a formal and shared conceptualization of a domain, the ontology is a computable knowledge base that can formalize relevant bits of information pertaining to that domain [17]. Ontology emerged as one of the cornerstones of Semantic Web in early 1990s, and it is nowadays adopted as the backbone of DSSs [18]. In fact, formal models are increasingly recognized among the key enablers of innovation in different health-related industries, where the possibility to rely on formalized expert knowledge can enhance cooperation, support common understanding and information exchange, orient decision-making [10, 19, 20]. Ontologies are modelled with languages based on Description Logic (DL) [21], which is powerful enough to enable concepts and relationships representation while enabling the generation of inferred knowledge through the use of reasoning programs.

The development of domain ontologies is usually conducted in a cooperative way to elicit all relevant knowledge and facts related to a domain—especially in health-related contexts, in which knowledge elicitation is fundamental [22]. Considering the peculiar involvement of different stakeholders in HEALPS2, the ontology engineering activity followed a collaborative and agile approach to identify, elicit and formalize all the relevant information from the domains addressed by the project (as described in the following Section) [23]. The result of this process consists in a knowledge map of the Alpine health tourism in which different tourism destination can recognize their features and, potentially, produce a self-description. With the use of automated reasoning, destinations' input data are processed to deliver tailored suggestions on which natural resources to exploit (and how to exploit them) in order to enhance the destinations' competitiveness in the Alpine health tourism industry.

4 Engineering and Use of the HEALPS2 Ontology

This Section describes the collaborative approach adopted for the identification and elicitation of the information to be formalized in the HEALPS2 ontology. Also, the conceptualization and development phase are further addressed in its subsections. The ontology engineering methodology adopted for developing the project's ontology is UPONLite [24], since it foresees non-experts in the field of Semantic Web to adopt common tools to provide a conceptualization of different domains of knowledge. UPONLite is an "agile" engineering methodology, i.e. it presents a non-rigid structure for knowledge elicitation and conceptualization activities: considering the high number of stakeholders involved in the project, an agile ontology engineering methodology suits best with the necessity of gathering domain insights from many sources [9, 23]. Specifically, developers and domain experts were involved into three main phases: Domain analysis, Domain conceptualization, Implementation and development.

4.1 Knowledge Elicitation for Domain Analysis

The ontology engineering process in UPONLite starts with the identification and definition of the concepts and relationships (i.e. lexicon and glossary) of the domain. In HEALPS2, the knowledge elicitation process is essential to get relevant concepts and relationships. Often mentioned as a bottleneck for ontology engineering [25], knowledge elicitation is a very delicate and time-consuming activity. Taken into account the high number of stakeholders involved in the project, informal and formal methods were conveniently adopted to ease achieving specific goals, such as identifying the most relevant bits of knowledge and produce an accessible and shared conceptual model to be developed into an ontology.

As mentioned in the Preface of this book [1], HEALPS2 research project fosters the collaboration among various stakeholders throughout the whole health tourism values chain. Thus, the involvement of these stakeholders in the knowledge elicitation activities covers an essential role to ensure capturing relevant information, and get relevant concepts and relationships. Stakeholders' ideas, opinions and knowledge were elicited through six national stakeholders' meetings (three held online due to pandemics' restrictions, and three held respectively in Austria, France, Slovenia, with the average participation of 15 stakeholders each) and one international stakeholders meeting (held online, with the participation of over 50 stakeholders). The purpose of these meetings was to select the concepts and relationships of interest in the Alpine health tourism domain of knowledge, and to agree on a definition for each of them. By leveraging on the KPI model [26] and on HEALPS2 project partners' support, data collected were transformed in quantifiable KPIs—which contributed to build the base concept and relationship model.

The relevant concepts and relationships elicited during the stakeholders' meetings were then put together into a conceptual map, which also encompassed KPIs descriptions. As foreseen by the methodology, stakeholders made use of different and familiar tools to made their ideas and opinions explicit, including unstructured interviews, brainstorming, active discussions, spreadsheets and documents.

4.2 Domain Conceptualization

While the domain analysis phase relied heavily on stakeholders' knowledge, the subsequent conceptualization phase leveraged more on project partners' inputs. In particular, the KPI model [26] was integrated in the conceptualization of the domain, since it provides a common and agreed framework to capture relevant information on the tourism destinations. The information was represented in the form of a conceptual map (Fig. 1), in which the main concepts and relationships were discussed and defined.

The domains elicited in the previous phase were multiple. From a health tourism perspective, the main groups of patients who could benefit from nature-based health

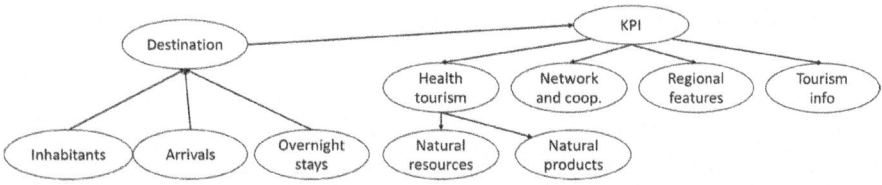

Fig. 1 An excerpt of the conceptual map deriving from the domain conceptualization phase

tourism in the Alpine space were identified. Similarly, the medical but also the health economic and tourism perspectives consider important to know which natural resources can be used and in which way—i.e., which products and services can be provided. There are also relevant quantitative indicators regarding the tourists' arrival, their overnight stay and provenance, to assess the tourism inflow in a specific tourism destination.

The result of the Domain analysis and Conceptualization phases brought to the following concepts to be addressed:

- Target Groups (TGs): each corresponding to a group of tourists suffering from a chronic condition or physical limitations, for which nature-based health tourism activity can provide benefits (e.g.: lack of mobility, diabetes and metabolic disorders, skin conditions, exhaustion and tiredness, etc.).
- Tourism in general: a concept in which data describing a specific tourism destination and its touristic inflow are detailed (tourists' arrivals, their country of origin, duration of stays, tourists' age and gender, destination population density, economic impact of tourism on the destination—tourism intensity, overnight stays per 1000 inhabitants).
- Natural Resources: a concept divided into the main natural resources populating the Alpine space (blue spaces, forests, waterfalls, altitudes, protected areas, specific flora), their products (mineral waters, nature-based local products such as Alpine dairy products, farm products, honey, etc.), and essential indicators to assess the degree of environmental pollution through a set of metrics (air pollution, light pollution, noise pollution).
- Regional Features: a set of descriptive concepts that identifies and defines the main characteristics of a health tourism destination, also listing the services it can provide (e.g.: health manager, nutritional advice, mountain hiking activities, spa treatments, physiotherapy, etc.); some services are correlated with the availability of one or more natural resources.
- Cooperation and Networking: a success factor for health tourism destinations was identified in the opportunities to participate in cooperative networks (regional, national or international).

After identifying these the concepts and their features, KPIs were linked to each domain feature to allow the ontology to quantify data regarding tourism destination and their services, as well as the existence and use of natural resources.

4.3 Implementation and Development

The conceptual model containing the logical and mathematical relationships among concepts was implemented into an ontology using the Protégé ontology editor [27]. Resource Description Framework (RDF) [28] and Ontology Web Language (OWL) [29] were adopted as ontological languages, with rules written in Semantic Web Rule Language (SWRL) [30]. The HEALPS2 ontology encompasses more than 85

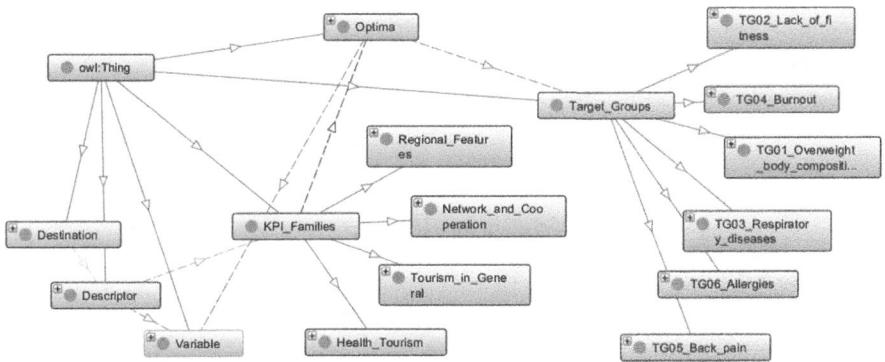

Fig. 2 A graphical representation of the main concepts composing the HEALPS2 ontology's taxonomy and their relationships (generated with Protégé ontology editor)

classes, 9 object properties, 57 datatype properties and includes 1075 individuals (for a total of 7265 axioms, including SWRL rules). Figure 2 shows an excerpt of the taxonomy of the developed ontology.

The DL consistency of the ontology was checked with the Pellet reasoner [31], as it is one of the few reasoners able to process SWRL built-in functions (necessary to state mathematical relationships among concepts). The ontology prefix is "hlp".

4.4 Using HEALPS2 Ontology to Represent Health Tourism Destinations

The set of KPIs necessary for describing a destination in the ontology is represented by four classes (hlp : Health_tourism, hlp : Network_and_Cooperation, hlp : Regional_features, hlp : Tourism_in_General). Each of these classes is further specified by subclasses. The ontology allows representing a health tourism destination as an OWL individual belonging to the class hlp : Destination. Each destination is described by a set of hlp : Descriptors (one for each KPI, for a total of 56 descriptors), which hlp : quantifies a specific KPI. Using this pattern, it is possible to assert that a destination can count on a specific natural resource (hlp : exists), which can (or cannot) be currently used for tourism purposes (hlp : use) and which can generate health-related natural products (hlp : product), as shown in Fig. 3.

The TGs are also represented in HEALPS2 ontology as classes and individuals. Each of the TG is linked to a KPI and an optimum value—i.e. the degree to which a specific destination feature (natural resource, product, service, etc.) can help or intervene on the health issue represented by the TG—is stated (as illustrated in Fig. 4).

68 D. Spoladore and E. Pessot

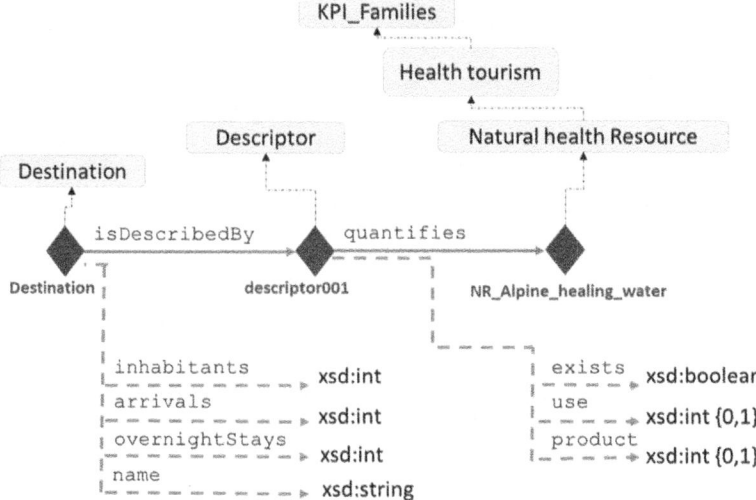

Fig. 3 An excerpt of the HEALPS2 ontology illustrating the modelling of a destination and the representation of a KPI (labelled rectangles represent classes; diamonds indicate individuals; dashed arrows indicate datatype properties, full-line arrows indicate object properties; the rdf:type of an individual is stated with a dotted arrow)

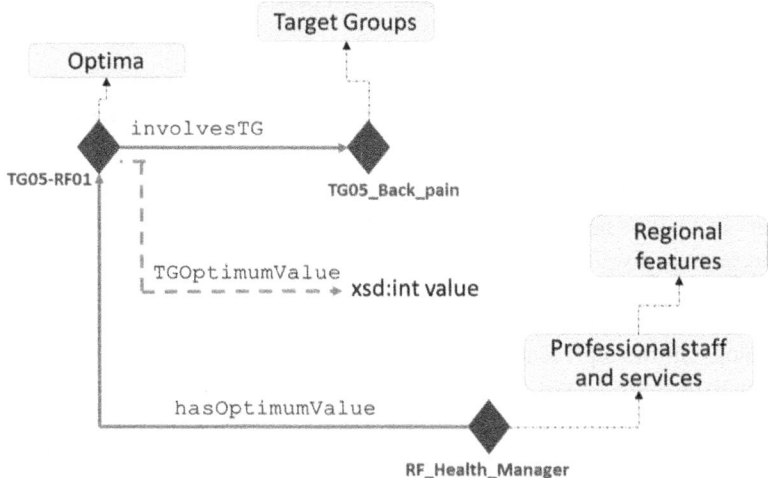

Fig. 4 The representation of an optimum for a TG. The "importance" of having a health manager for people characterized by back pain is stated through an integer value (ranging from a minimum of 1 to a maximum of 10)

Fig. 5 The score (hlp : VAR_value) inferred for a variable associated to a TG and a descriptor (generated using Pellet reasoner)

Each destination, described and valorized by its descriptors, is then compared with the values depicted for the optima using SWRL rules. Through a reasoning process, the results of the comparison processes are then further elaborated attributing scores to the destination, and are finally stored in individual variables (Fig. 5). The scores—which are delivered to the application, as described in Chap. 5 [11]—indicate the preliminary level of adequacy of the tourism destination for specific TGs.

The DSS is therefore able to calculate the differences occurring between the optimum values for each TGs and the effective values hold by a destination: in this way, the ontology supports the identification of those natural resources and/or services worth investing on. To populate the ontology and test the SWRL rules, project partners were to provide four Alpine health destinations and their information.

5 Conclusions and Future Works

This Chapter presented an ontology-based DSS to support NTH destinations in innovating and enriching their product offerings by leveraging on local natural resources. Specifically, it describes the collaborative engineering process and delves into the ontology's structure as its result, highlighting how it can contribute in identifying the natural resources or services to be exploited for enhancing the nature-based health tourism offer of destinations. The DSS also provides an example of knowledge-based digital tool for Alpine health tourism, and its results are further adopted by an application specifically dedicated for destination managers and policy makers.

References

1. D. Spoladore, E. Pessot, M. Sacco, A. Hartl, C. Pichler, Preface. in *Digital and strategic innovation for Alpine health tourism* (Springer 2022)
2. G.C. Steckenbauer, S. Tischler, A. Hartl, C. Pichler, Destination and product development rested on evidence-based health tourism. in *The Routledge Handbook of Health Tourism* (2017), pp. 315–331
3. C. Grafetstätter, M. Gaisberger, J. Prossegger, M. Ritter, P. Kolarž, C. Pichler, J. Thalhamer, A. Hartl, Does waterfall aerosol influence mucosal immunity and chronic stress? A randomized controlled clinical trial. J. Physiol. Anthropol. **36**, 1–12 (2017)
4. A. Pieroni, M.E. Giusti, Alpine ethnobotany in Italy: traditional knowledge of gastronomic and medicinal plants among the Occitans of the upper Varaita valley Piedmont. J. Ethnobiol. Ethnomed. **5**, 1–13 (2009)
5. J. Prossegger, D. Huber, C. Grafetstätter, C. Pichler, R. Weisböck-Erdheim, B. Iglseder, G. Wewerka, A. Hartl, Effects of moderate mountain hiking and balneotherapy on community-dwelling older people: A randomized controlled trial. Exp. Gerontol. **122**, 74–84 (2019)
6. C. Pichler, A. Hartl, R. Weisböck-Erdheim, M. Bischof, Medical evidence of Alpine natural resources as a base for health tourism. in *Digital and Strategic Innovation for Alpine Health Tourism—Natural Resources, Digital Tools and Innovation Practices from HEALPS 2 Project*, ed. by D. Spoladore, E. Pessot, M. Sacco (Springer 2023)
7. E. Pessot, D. Spoladore, A. Zangiacomi, M. Sacco, Natural resources in health tourism: a systematic literature review. Sustainability **13**, 2661 (2021)
8. B.K.M. Wong, S.A.S. Hazley, The future of health tourism in the industrial revolution 4.0 era. J. Tourism Futures (2020)
9. D. Spoladore, E. Pessot, M. Bischof, A. Hartl, M. Sacco, Collaborative design approach for the development of an ontology-based decision support system in health tourism. in *Working Conference on Virtual Enterprises* (Springer 2021), pp. 632–639
10. D. Spoladore, M. Sacco, Towards a collaborative ontology-based decision support system to foster healthy and tailored diets. in *Working Conference on Virtual Enterprises* (Springer 2020), pp. 634–643
11. A. Mahroo, D. Spoladore, P. Ferrandi, I. Lovato, A digital application for strategic development of health tourism destinations. in *Digital and Strategic Innovation for Alpine Health Tourism - Natural Resources, Digital Tools and Innovation Practices from HEALPS 2 Project*, ed. by D. Spoladore, E. Pessot, M. Sacco (Springer 2023)
12. J. Lu, D. Wu, M. Mao, W. Wang, G. Zhang, Recommender system application developments: a survey. Decis. Support Syst. **74**, 12–32 (2015)
13. C. Chantrapornchai, C. Choksuchat, Ontology construction and application in practice case study of health tourism in Thailand. Springerplus **5**, 1–31 (2016)
14. H. Khallouki, A. Abatal, M. Bahaj, An ontology-based context awareness for smart tourism recommendation system. in *Proceedings of the International Conference on Learning and Optimization Algorithms: Theory and Applications* (2018), pp. 1–5
15. M. Frikha, M. Mhiri, F. Gargouri et al. A semantic social recommender system using ontologies based approach for Tunisian tourism. (2015)
16. H.J. Lee, S.Y. Park, H.R. Jin, M. Sohn, A smart orchestrator of ecosystem in medical tourism. in *Proceedings of the 18th Annual International Conference on Electronic Commerce: e-Commerce in Smart connected World* (2016), pp. 1–8
17. T.R. Gruber, A translation approach to portable ontology specifications. Knowl. Acquis. **5**, 199–220 (1993)
18. E. Blomqvist, The use of semantic web technologies for decision support–a survey. Semant. Web. **5**, 177–201 (2014)
19. D. Spoladore, S. Arlati, S. Carciotti, M. Nolich, M. Sacco, RoomFort: an ontology-based comfort management application for hotels. Electronics **7**, 345 (2018)

20. D. Spoladore, S. Arlati, V. Colombo, G. Modoni, M. Sacco, A semantic-enabled smart home for AAL and continuity of care. in *IoT in Healthcare and Ambient Assisted Living.*. (Springer 2021), pp. 343–371
21. F. Baader, I. Horrocks, U. Sattler, Description logics. in *Handbook on Ontologies* (Springer 2004), pp. 3–28
22. D. Spoladore, E. Pessot, Collaborative ontology engineering methodologies for the development of decision support systems: Case studies in the healthcare domain. Electronics **10**, 1060 (2021)
23. D. Spoladore, E. Pessot, An evaluation of agile ontology engineering methodologies for the digital transformation of companies. Comput. Ind. **140**, 103690 (2022)
24. A. De Nicola, M. Missikoff, A lightweight methodology for rapid ontology engineering. Commun. ACM **59**, 79–86 (2016)
25. F. Hayes-Roth, D.A. Waterman, D.B. Lenat, *Building expert systems* (Addison-Wesley Longman Publishing Co., Inc. 1983)
26. M. Bischof, A. Hartl, KPI for data-driven assessment of innovative development paths for nature-based health tourism in the Alpine region. in *Digital and Strategic Innovation for Alpine Health Tourism—Natural Resources, Digital Tools and Innovation Practices from HEALPS 2 Project* D. Spoladore, E. Pessot, M. Sacco (Springer 2023)
27. T. Tudorache, N.F. Noy, S. Tu, M.A. Musen, Supporting collaborative ontology development in Protégé. in *International Semantic Web Conference* (Springer 2008), pp. 17–32
28. J.Z. Pan, Resource description framework. in *Handbook on Ontologies* (Springer 2009), pp. 71–90
29. G. Antoniou, F. Van Harmelen, Web ontology language: Owl. in *Handbook on Ontologies* (Springer 2004), pp. 67–92
30. I. Horrocks, P.F. Patel-Schneider, H. Boley, S. Tabet, B. Grosof, M. Dean et al., SWRL: A semantic web rule language combining OWL and ruleML. W3C Member Submission **21**, 1–31 (2004)
31. E. Sirin, B. Parsia, B. C. Grau, A. Kalyanpur, Y. Katz, Pellet: A practical owl-dl reasoner. Journal of Web Semantics, **5**(2), 51–53 (2007)

Open Access This chapter is licensed under the terms of the Creative Commons Attribution 4.0 International License (http://creativecommons.org/licenses/by/4.0/), which permits use, sharing, adaptation, distribution and reproduction in any medium or format, as long as you give appropriate credit to the original author(s) and the source, provide a link to the Creative Commons license and indicate if changes were made.

The images or other third party material in this chapter are included in the chapter's Creative Commons license, unless indicated otherwise in a credit line to the material. If material is not included in the chapter's Creative Commons license and your intended use is not permitted by statutory regulation or exceeds the permitted use, you will need to obtain permission directly from the copyright holder.

A Digital Application for Strategic Development of Health Tourism Destinations

Atieh Mahroo, Daniele Spoladore, Paolo Ferrandi, and Ilenia Lovato

Abstract This work describes the challenges, techniques, and methodologies to develop a digital tool that aims to improve framework conditions and tools for better utilization of Alpine natural resources in health tourism. Starting from the literature analysis and an online survey, the system implemented a comprehensive knowledge base adopted for an ontology-based Decision Support System leveraging on identified Key Performance Indicators (KPIs). Relying on this knowledge, the digital tool provides a list of tailored and customized recommendations for each destination within the Alpine area. This result helps the stakeholders capitalize on the nature-based health tourism potentials of their region in relation to the existence of the natural resources and different target users' health conditions. This strategic digital tool is developed as a web-based application for destinations' policy-makers and managers to fill the online survey and receive customized suggestions, recommendations, and insights on how to further exploit their natural resources in order to enhance nature-based health tourism.

Keywords Health tourism · Natural resources · Nature-based tourism · Wellness tourism · Decision support system · Alpine region

---

A. Mahroo (✉) · D. Spoladore
Institute of Intelligent Industrial Technologies and Systems for Advanced Manufacturing (STIIMA) National Research Council of Italy, Lecco, Italy
e-mail: atieh.mahroo@stiima.cnr.it

D. Spoladore
e-mail: daniele.spoladore@stiima.cnr.it

D. Spoladore
Department of Pure and Applied Sciences, Insubria University, Varese, Italy

P. Ferrandi · I. Lovato
Moxoff Spa, Milan, Italy
e-mail: paolo.ferrandi@moxoff.com

I. Lovato
e-mail: ilenia.lovato@moxoff.com

© The Author(s) 2023
D. Spoladore et al. (eds.), *Digital and Strategic Innovation for Alpine Health Tourism*, SpringerBriefs in Applied Sciences and Technology,
https://doi.org/10.1007/978-3-031-15457-7_5

1 Introduction

This Chapter presents the results of research activities conducted to develop a digital application for the strategic development of evidence and nature-based health tourism (NHT) destinations. The Health Tourism Assessment and Benchmarking (HTAB) tool aims to provide customized recommendations for developing health tourism products in Alpine destinations in order to further exploit the NHT market.

Tourism is a major force for economic growth, job creation, and sustainable development in the Alpine area. Additionally, nature-based experiences and products are increasingly growing due to their known benefits on people's physical and mental health. This trend brings substantial opportunities for developing innovative NHT knowledge and implementation tools in the Alpine regions.

Health tourism is a type of tourism in which people travel to specific destinations in order to receive particular medical treatments or enhance their physical/mental health and general well-being [1, 2]. Health tourism is divided into three different yet overlapping components: medical tourism, wellness tourism, and spa tourism [3]. While medical tourism foresees traveling to a particular destination to access medical treatment, wellness tourism is associated with traveling to maintain, strengthen, and rejuvenate the tourists' physical or mental health [4]. Spa tourism, however, is the intersection of medical and wellness tourism to combine the medical treatment and healing process together.

Wellness tourism is a broad concept, and its meaning depends on the geography and culture of each tourism destination. While in southern Europe, wellness tourism is associated with the seaside and Mediterranean culture, it is more connected to swimming and hiking in northern Europe. Alpine regions appear to be among the most popular health travel destinations for rewarding elements such as indulgence, leisure, and regeneration, combined with more challenging and stimulating elements, including outdoor activities and sports (hiking, mountain biking, and golf) [5]. The unique Alpine natural resources such as healing waters, forests, and waterfalls play a significant role in the exploitation and sustainability of health tourism in Alpine destinations. Identifying these potential assets and resources in different regions within the Alpine area can lead the regional stakeholders and policy-makers to further cooperate and reap the benefits of a new value chain [6].

In this context, this Chapter investigates the development of the HTAB tool based on the ontology implemented within the Decision Support System (DSS) described in Chap. 4 [7] to identify the natural resources of different Alpine destinations and provide customized recommendations accordingly. Starting from an online survey filled by the destination, the HTAB tool cleans, processes, and translates the data into a semantic representation of the domain knowledge to reason and infer the output results. The HTAB tool results are then sent to the destination managers to be used by tourism stakeholders to better understand the potential of their region and the specific resources and products to capitalize on.

The remainder of this Chapter is organized as follows: Sect. 2 underlines some of the remarkable studies in the context of health tourism and digital applications;

Sect. 3 highlights the process of domain knowledge elicitation and formalization; Sect. 4 discusses the detailed architecture and pipeline of the HTAB tool; and finally, Sect. 5 concludes the main outcomes of the project.

2 Related Work

Health tourism has been around throughout history; however, the research and literature study on this topic has grown extensively over the last few decades [3]. Many cities around Europe have started to invest in their available resources to position themselves as health destinations and attract health-conscious tourists [1]. Study shows that some destinations utilize natural resources such as healing waters and clean air to promote health tourism and the local economy [8, 9]. Natural resources may include the existence of the physical natural features (such as lakes, mountains, waterfalls, and forests), the derived products (like local food and sports classes), and regional cultural heritage [10].

As a result of this growing opportunity in health tourism, the adoption of new technologies such as DSS, semantic knowledge implementation, and digital tools and applications to exploit the local resources are also rising. The implementation of semantic technologies and ontologies for a medical tourism recommender system has been investigated in the work of Frikha et al. [11]. Moreover, a DSS was developed in another study [12] to evaluate the key factors such as climate, tourism development, and attractions to propose a hierarchical structure for rating the destinations.

Exploiting the semantic reasoning and ontologies, Moreno et al. [13] developed a web-based platform to provide personalized recommendations for touristic and leisure activities based on demographics, motivations, user actions, and ratings. In another example of an ontology-based application [14], researchers created a novel health tourism ontology and built a semantic web-based search application for health tourism in Thailand.

This work presents a digital web-based application to provide customized recommendations to destination stakeholders and tourism policy-makers in order to offer insights and suggestions on how to further exploit the health tourism industry by investing in their natural resources. This digital application relies on an ontology-based DSS (described in Chap. 4 [7]), which formalizes the representation of health tourism destinations, their natural resources, services, and activities based on the natural resources.

3 Knowledge Implementation

Prior to the development of the digital tool, adopting a collaborative approach to implement and elicit the domain knowledge is a vital step. As described in the previous Chapter, within the HEALPS2 project, the process of formalizing the information is performed through the collaboration among various stakeholders from six countries to capture their ideas, knowledge, and opinions in the process of knowledge elicitation. Data collected from the research studies, unstructured interviews, and stakeholders' brainstorming was then transformed into quantifiable Key Performance Indicators (KPIs), which later formed the basic roadmap toward semantic model formalization.

3.1 Defining KPIs

In order to provide a set of tailored recommendations, some general KPIs have been identified to further emphasize the importance of the natural resources of each destination [15]. The existence of one or more natural resources, which are known to have a positive impact on particular health conditions, can lead to a more precise approach toward improving health tourism in a given destination. The KPIs are defined considering the existence of the natural resources and general framework of tourism in every destination in order to receive a set of customized suggestions on the target group, products, and natural resources to exploit. The process of selecting the KPIs in Alpine health tourism is discussed in detail in Chap. 3 [15].

3.2 Semantic Representation

The information gathered from the KPIs is then further formalized in a semantic data model representing the knowledge regarding the tourist destinations, the existence of the natural resources, target groups, and the relationship between all these factors [16]. A semantic approach can support data integration by annotating and enriching the unstructured and semi-structured data coming from the KPIs and online surveys. The semantic model is expressed as a set of ontologies, i.e., "formal, explicit specifications of a shared conceptualization" [17], modeled with Resource Description Framework (RDF) [18] and Web Ontology Language (OWL) [19], while reasoning and data inference are accomplished with the Semantic Web Rule Language (SWRL) [20] and SPARQL Protocol and RDF Query Language (SPARQL) [21].

Together with the SWRL, the ontology is then stored on Stardog [22]—a commercial RDF database with fast SPARQL query, transactions, and OWL reasoning support. Once the ontology is available on the Stardog server, the HTAB digital tool is able to exploit the semantic repository, reason the knowledge domain, and infer new data. The structure of the semantic model and the ontology defined to be used within the HTAB tool is discussed in detail in Chap. 4 [7].

4 The HTAB Tool Pipeline

The HTAB tool is a web-based digital application that triggers a pipeline behind the web platform. The synergy between a web-based application and ontology-based approaches is widely documented in the literature, and some examples can also be traced in the tourism industry [23, 24]. The pipeline receives data, preprocesses and cleans the data, exchanges and translates the data into a semantic representation of the HEALPS2 data model, and produces the output results with recommendations and suggestions for the destination (Fig. 1). The HTAB tool is implemented on the Paracelsus Medical University (PMU) server to run automatically every day and verify if there is any new answer to the online questionnaire on the Lime Survey platform [25]. If a new questionnaire answer is found, the HTAB tool starts the pipeline by gathering the input data, reasoning and querying the semantic knowledge, and finally dispatching the output results to the destination. These steps of the HTAB digital application and its pipeline are discussed in detail in the following subsections.

4.1 Gathering Input Data

The HTAB tool runs based on the input data coming from the online questionnaire, to which a destination must answer in order to receive the recommendations. These input data should then be collected, cleaned, and translated to add value to the DSS to be reasoned and infer the output results.

Online Survey. The online questionnaire is hosted on Lime Survey available in five languages: English, French, German, Italian, and Slovenian. Each Alpine destination can fill the questionnaire directly on the Lime Survey platform and provide their email address to which the output results will be sent later. The survey consists of 25 questions divided into the subtopics as follows:

- General information on the region such as number of inhabitants, number of tourists, tourists' countries of origin;
- Presence and use of some natural health resources such as waterfalls, forests, healing waters;
- Presence of some health tourism services such as health checks, physiotherapy, bicycle availability; and
- Cooperation with stakeholders and membership in tourism networks and tourism attractions.

The questionnaire's answers are retrieved and downloaded once the application is launched through the HTTP POST method of the REST API. This process is implemented and automated via a Python script to fetch the questionnaire's answers from the Lime Survey platform and then decode and translate the collected data into CSV format. Consequently, the CSV data is easily imported and stored in the database.

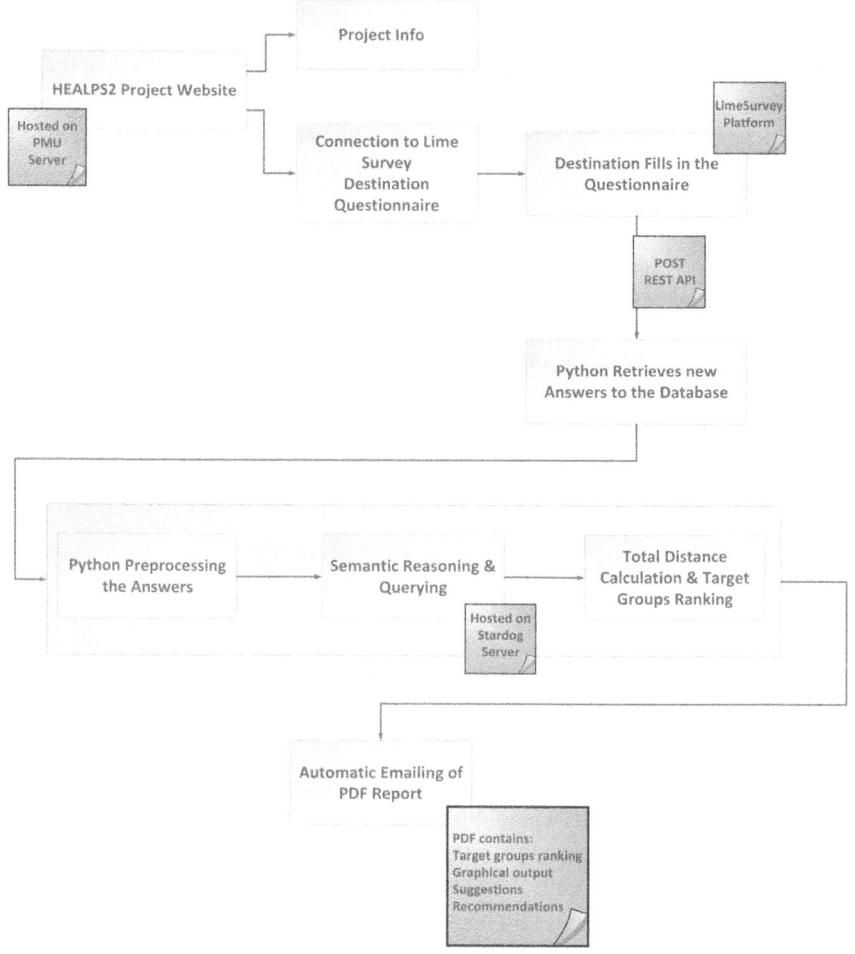

Fig. 1 The pipeline behind the HTAB web-based application to receive and preprocess input data, query and infer reasoned data, and dispatch the output data

Data Preprocessing. Since the data coming from the online questionnaire is not machine-readable and therefore not in the required format to be used in the semantic model, it is necessary to preprocess and encode the data before sending it to the semantic database. Firstly, the data from the questionnaire must be mapped to the associated KPIs defined earlier, considering that each question within the online survey may refer to one or more KPIs. The data downloaded from the Lime Survey and stored in the database are identified with coded column names, while the KPIs are defined with another coding system. Therefore, a mapping table is implemented in Python to match the questions with the database column names and associated KPIs.

Moreover, the given answers to the questionnaire must be decoded according to the expected machine-readable answers. As a result, another mapping table is implemented to define and specify all the real answers and their associated machine-readable codes. Also, some questions may have more complicated textual or imagery answers that must be translated to numerical values.

Input JSON File Generating for Semantic Reasoning. Once the questionnaire's results are decoded, cleaned, and in a correct machine-readable format, the data regarding the destination must be written in a JSON file to be readable for the semantic model. Therefore, a JSON file is generated via Python, which includes all the necessary data in a format that is consistent with the semantic model and the ontology. The JSON file contains the information about a destination together with the necessary datatype properties and the descriptors defined in the ontology (Fig. 2). All these JSON attributes must be filled in via Python dictionary by extracting the required information from the preprocessed survey answers. The JSON file generated at this stage will be saved on the server to be used by the semantic repository in the next phase.

```
{
        "Destination":
        {
                "name": "Valposchiavo",
                "arrivals": "30000",
                "overnightStays": "55000",
                "inhabitants": "4500",
                "isSelected": "true"},
                "Descriptors":
                {
                        "descValposchiavo_55":
                        {
                                "key1": "9",
                                "key2": "4",
                                "key3": "7"
                        },
```

Fig. 2 An excerpt of the JSON file generated from the data coming from the questionnaire that is served as input to insert the new destination "Valposchiavo" into the semantic model

4.2 Reasoning and Querying Inferred Output Data (Java Middleware)

In order to receive the customized recommendation and suggestions regarding each destination and target group, HTAB is capable of connecting to the semantic repository, running the reasoner, and retrieving the inferred data. Moreover, the scalability of the digital tool relies on the possibility of adding new destinations to the system in the future. However, there are some limitations imposed by the Open-World Assumption (OWA) of the monotonic nature of Description Logic (DL). OWL exploits the OWA reasoning technique in which it cannot assume something does not exist unless it is explicitly stated [26]. Therefore, it is impossible for the deductive reasoner to infer the existence of a new instance unless it is already modeled in the semantic knowledge base. Hence, inserting a new piece of information into the semantic repository is not a task supported by DL-based technologies [27, 28]. As a result, the HTAB tool relies on a Java application acting as a middleware [29, 30] between the digital tool and the semantic repository to clear these barriers.

This Java application runs the Stardog server, creates a semantic database, and uploads the ontology files on the server. The Java application also defines the reasoning type needed to be exploited on this particular knowledge base according to the DL rules. At this point, the knowledge base is up and running on the Stardog repository, the SWRL rules are translated and consistent with the Stardog to infer data, and the reasoning logic to infer new pieces of information is set.

The Java application is now ready to receive the information about the new destination produced from the online survey. All the necessary information about a new destination is generated, cleaned, and incorporated into a JSON file (Sect. 4.1). The application fetches the JSON file to extract the information and generates a proper SPARQL query to insert the new destination into the knowledge base. The query must conform according to the data types defined in the ontology regarding each attribute while including all the necessary descriptors characterizing each destination in order not to cause any inconsistency within the knowledge base. The Java middleware utilizes a mapping table to associate each destination's descriptor to the corresponding KPIs defined within the semantic database and the ontology to keep the data consistency. The application translates the JSON information into a correct *INSERT* SPARQL query and runs the query against the Stardog query system to append the new destination data into the knowledge base (Fig. 3).

The ontology on the Stardog semantic repository is now updated with the new destination information; hence, the knowledge can be reasoned according to the predefined rules and reasoning techniques. The Java application then generates the proper SELECT SPARQL query to retrieve the inferred data regarding the new destination recommendations. The query then runs on the Stardog server with DL reasoning techniques to infer data based on each target group. In fact, the reasoner is run once for each target group to calculate the correct optimal value for the specific health condition the target group entails. Each target group represents a group of tourists suffering from physical limitations or chronic conditions such as respiratory

```
prefix HEALPS2: <http://www.stiima.cnr.it/Healps2KPImodel#>
INSERT data
{
        HEALPS2:Valposchiavo rdf:type HEALPS2:Destination;
                     rdf:type owl:NamedIndividual;
                     HEALPS2:name 'Valposchiavo';
                     HEALPS2:inhabitants 4500;
                     HEALPS2:arrivals 30000;
                     HEALPS2:overnightStays 55000;
                     HEALPS2:isSelected true;
                     HEALPS2:isDescribedBy :descValposchiavo_55.
        HEALPS2:descValposchiavo_55 rdf:type HEALPS2:Descriptor;
                     rdf:type owl:NamedIndividual;
                     HEALPS2:quantifies HEALPS2:RF_Image;
                     HEALPS2:hasD_ID 55;
                     HEALPS2:key1 9 ;
                     HEALPS2:key2 4 ;
                     HEALPS2:key3 7 .
        HEALPS2:RF_Image   rdf:type HEALPS2:Network_participation.
}
```

Fig. 3 An excerpt of the SPARQL *INSERT* query to insert the new destination "Valposchiavo" into the semantic model together with its attributes

diseases or allergies in which it is associated with an optimum value to demonstrate how much the health condition described within the target group can be enhanced by a specific destination natural resources and products. The application retrieves the reasoned results from the semantic repository through the reasoning process, which illustrates the optimum values for each target group for the new destination. The process of choosing different target groups and calculating the optimal values is discussed in detail in Chap. 4 [7].

Once the reasoning for every target group is done, the application generates the output JSON files integrating the results (Fig. 4). The results are divided into separate JSON files for each target group, providing reasoned information based on each target group's health conditions and their respective optimal values.

4.3 Dispatching the Output Results

Once the inferred and reasoned results are generated in JSON files, the system is ready to calculate the target group ranking and dispatch the final output for the destination. In order to calculate the ranking for the destination, the values related to the KPIs are extracted from the output JSON files and multiplied by the predefined weights associated with KPIs. These weighted values are then aggregated and compared with an optimal value specific for each target group. A ranking among target groups is then created, sorting their final scores in descending order.

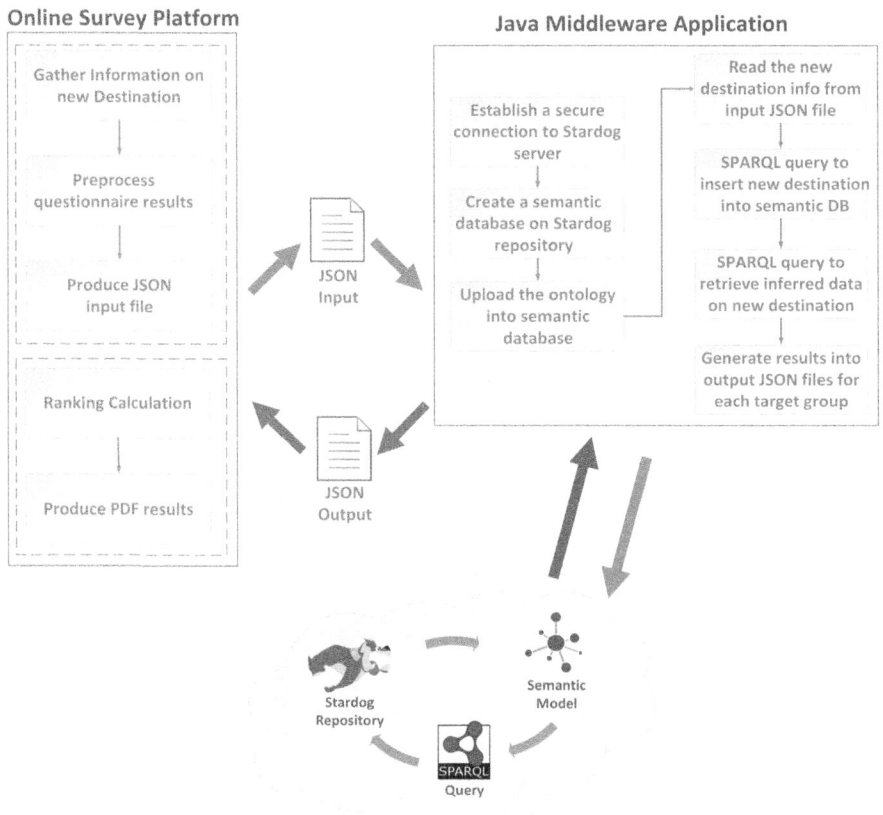

Fig. 4 Conceptual architecture of the HTAB digital pipeline and the interactions between the semantic middleware with semantic repository and the input/output data

The final output is a report, provided as a PDF file generated dynamically via Python, which consists of an introduction, medical evidence, recommendations, natural resources and services, key figures on the importance of tourism, cooperation and networks, and additional illustrative figures. The PDF file is the final output of the HTAB pipeline that provides necessary information and insights for the destination to improve their tourism resources, products, and policies to better exploit the health tourism within their region.

This PDF report is automatically sent to the email address the destination provided on the Lime survey to fill the questionnaire.

5 Conclusion

This Chapter presented the architecture of the HTAB digital tool to support the Alpine destinations in further exploiting their natural resources in health tourism. Starting from literature to understand the impacts of the Alpine natural resources on tourists' physical and mental health [31], the project defined a comprehensive list of success factors through collaboration among various stakeholders. This Chapter describes how the HTAB digital tool is developed to identify the destination's tourism characteristics and utilize this data in order to provide tailored and customized suggestions to the destination to exploit the NHT industry of the destination. The digital application retrieves the data about each Alpine destination through an online survey; cleans, preprocesses, and encodes the data; reasons and queries the data against the domain knowledge base; and finally provides a set of customized suggestions and recommendations to the destination manager.

References

1. L. Chang, R. Beise-Zee, Consumer perception of healthfulness and appraisal of health-promoting tourist destinations. Tourism Rev. (2013)
2. J.Y. Yang, S. Paek, T.T. Kim, T.H. Lee, Health tourism: needs for healing experience and intentions for transformation in wellness resorts in Korea. Int. J. Contemp. Hospitality Manag. (2015)
3. C.M. Hall, Health and medical tourism: a kill or cure for global public health? Tourism review. (2011)
4. J. Connell, Contemporary medical tourism: conceptualisation, culture and commodification. Tour. Manage. **34**, 1–13 (2013)
5. C. Laesser, Health travel motivation and activities: insights from a mature market–Switzerland. Tourism Review. (2011)
6. C. Pichler, Healing Alps: Tourism based on natural health resources as strategic innovation for the development of Alpine regions. https://www.alpine-space.org/projects/healps-2/deliverables/d.m.1.1-healps-2-projet-management-handbook—pmh.pdf
7. D. Spoladore, E. Pessot, An ontology-based decision support system to foster innovation and competitiveness opportunities of health tourism destinations. in *Digital and Strategic Innovation for Alpine Health Tourism - Natural Resources, Digital Tools and Innovation Practices from HEALPS 2 Project* D. Spoladore, E. Pessot, M. Sacco (Springer 2023)
8. E. Kušen et al., Health tourism. Tourism (Zagreb). **50**, 175–188 (2002)
9. E. Pessot, D. Spoladore, A. Zangiacomi, M. Sacco, Natural resources in health tourism: a systematic literature review. Sustainability **13**, 2661 (2021)
10. World tourism organization, European travel commission.: exploring health tourism—executive summary (2018)
11. M. Frikha, M. Mhiri, F. Gargouri et al., A semantic social recommender system using ontologies based approach for Tunisian tourism (2015)
12. E. Didascalou, D. Lagos, Wellness tourism: evaluating destination attributes for tourism planning in a competitive segment market. Tourismos. **4**, 113–126 (2009)
13. A. Moreno, A. Valls, D. Isern, L. Marin, J. Borràs, Sigtur/e-destination: ontology-based personalized recommendation of tourism and leisure activities. Eng. Appl. Artif. Intell. **26**, 633–651 (2013)

14. C. Choksuchat, C. Chantrapornchai, On the development of health tourism semantic web with its parallel engine. Int. J. Metadata Semant. Ontol. **11**, 16–28 (2016)
15. M. Bischof, A. Hartl, KPI for data-driven assessment of innovative development paths for nature-based health tourism in the Alpine region. in *Digital and Strategic Innovation for Alpine Health Tourism - Natural Resources, Digital Tools and Innovation Practices from HEALPS 2 Project*, ed. by D. Spoladore, E. essot, M. Sacco (Springer 2023)
16. D. Spoladore, E. Pessot, Bischof Michael, A. Hartl, M. Sacco, Collaborative design approach for the development of an ontology-based decision support system in health tourism. in *Working Conference on Virtual Enterprises* (Springer 2021), pp. 632–639
17. N. Guarino, D. Oberle, S. Staab, What is an ontology? in *Handbook on Ontologies* (Springer 2009), pp. 1–17
18. J.Z. Pan, Resource description framework. in *Handbook on Ontologies* (Springer 2009), pp. 71–90
19. D.L. McGuinness, F. Van Harmelen et al., OWL web ontology language overview. W3C recommendation. **10**, 2004 (2004)
20. I. Horrocks, P.F. Patel-Schneider, H. Boley, S. Tabet, B. Grosof, M. Dean et al., SWRL: a semantic web rule language combining OWL and RuleML. W3C Member submission. **21**, 1–31 (2004)
21. Eric Prud'hommeaux, A.S.: SPARQL Query Language for RDF. https://www.w3.org/TR/rdf-sparql-query/. (2008)
22. Stardog: Stardog. https://www.stardog.com/
23. P. Barsocchi, E. Ferro, D. La Rosa, A. Mahroo, D. Spoladore, E-Cabin: a software architecture for passenger comfort and cruise ship management. Sensors **19**, 4978 (2019)
24. A. Mahroo, Spoladore, D., Nolich, M., Buqi, R., Carciotti, S., Sacco, M.: Smart cabin: a semantic-based framework for indoor comfort customization inside a cruise cabin. in *Fourth International Congress on Information and Communication Technology* (Springer 2020), pp. 41–53
25. Lime Survey: Lime Survey. https://www.limesurvey.org/
26. F. Baader, I. Horrocks, U. Sattler, Description logics as ontology languages for the semantic web. in Mechanizing mathematical reasoning. (Springer 2005), pp. 228–248
27. D. Beimel, M. Peleg, Using OWL and SWRL to represent and reason with situation-based access control policies. Data Knowl. Eng. **70**, 596–615 (2011)
28. A. Mahroo, D. Spoladore, E.G. Caldarola, G.E. Modoni, M. Sacco, Enabling the smart home through a semantic-based context-aware system. in *2018 IEEE International Conference on Pervasive Computing and Communi-cations Workshops (PerCom Workshops)* (IEEE 2018), pp. 543–548
29. D. Spoladore, A. Mahroo, A. Trombetta, M. Sacco, ComfOnt: a semantic framework for indoor comfort and energy saving in smart homes. Electronics **8**, 1449 (2019)
30. D. Spoladore, A. Mahroo, A. Trom-betta, M. Sacco, DOMUS: A domestic ontology managed ubiquitous system. J. Ambient Intell Humanized Comput. 1–16 (2021)
31. C. Pichler, A. Hartl, R. Weisböck-Erdheim, M. Bischof, Medical evidence of Alpine natural resources as a base for health tourism. in *Digital and Strategic Innovation for Alpine Health Tourism - Natural Resources, Digital Tools and Innovation Practices from HEALPS 2 Project*, ed by D. Spoladore, E. Pessot, M. Sacco (Springer 2023)

Open Access This chapter is licensed under the terms of the Creative Commons Attribution 4.0 International License (http://creativecommons.org/licenses/by/4.0/), which permits use, sharing, adaptation, distribution and reproduction in any medium or format, as long as you give appropriate credit to the original author(s) and the source, provide a link to the Creative Commons license and indicate if changes were made.

The images or other third party material in this chapter are included in the chapter's Creative Commons license, unless indicated otherwise in a credit line to the material. If material is not included in the chapter's Creative Commons license and your intended use is not permitted by statutory regulation or exceeds the permitted use, you will need to obtain permission directly from the copyright holder.

A Methodology for Participatory Stakeholder Engagement in Nature-Based Health Tourism

Danilo Čeh, Mirjana Nenad, and Elena Pessot

Abstract Participatory stakeholder engagement in strategy-making, for industries such as Nature-based Health Tourism (NHT), enhances the delivery of more useful and applicable strategies, with also higher chances to reach intended goals if compared to conventional top-down planning processes. This chapter describes the methodology identified and carried out in the HEALPS2 project to efficiently reach and engage stakeholders of Alpine NHT and to form a stakeholder group at the transnational level (including the engagement of EU-level ac-tors and networks). Based on the Quadruple Helix concept, the methodology integrates a process of stakeholder engagement and endorsement along three steps; the identification of the key points and the problems to be tackled for a successful stakeholder engagement; and the development of Regional and Transnational Stakeholder Groups that extend to the cooperation with EU-wide networks. Developing health tourism products and service chains, and sustaining them with strategies and policies, is a complex undertaking. The adoption of the stakeholder engagement approaches throughout the HEALPS2 project showed that it is of utmost importance to properly identify, involve and communicate with the stakeholders who effectively complement the success of the project, and its outcomes, in enhancing NHT competitiveness.

Keywords Stakeholder involvement · Quadruple helix model · Health tourism

1 Introduction

International experiences in tourism and natural resources management demonstrated that participatory stakeholder engagement methods enhance the delivery of more useful and applicable strategies [1, 2]. The chances of reaching the goals are much

---

D. Čeh · M. Nenad (✉)
Scientific Research Centre Bistra Ptuj, Ptuj, Slovenia
e-mail: mirjana.nenad@bistra.si

E. Pessot
Institute of Intelligent Industrial Systems and Technologies for Advanced Manufacturing, National Research Council of Italy, Lecco, Italy

higher as compared to the conventional top-down planning process. Through the conventional method a concept is forced onto the stakeholders by the decision-makers, while in collaborative planning, the stakeholders can have a say about what they would need, what they find important or even crucial.

A further advantage of stakeholder involvement in the strategy-making process is that a broad range of stakeholders will gain good knowledge and will become well-informed about the planning process and the strategy, while their experience, knowledge, and expertise can be drawn upon, and their ideas utilized. A traditional strategy-making process is usually linear and prescriptive, meaning that the local government (or a subcontracted company) assesses the conditions, needs, and financial resources of the municipality, as well as the legal and other requirements. The detail of the assessment is often limited by the staff's time and capacity, as well as the difficulties of access to relevant information and data. Thus, strategies developed this way often are not (or only to a small extent) implemented. The real needs of the population/community/region often only become visible through the involvement of stakeholders. Moreover, the flexible, collaborative implementation of the goals is much more probable if those who will be affected and concretely make changes in their activities approve of the aims and objectives of the work plan. The mutual engagement with the participatory process will result in a better strategy, and the transparent, collaborative planning process will increase the willingness to cooperate and implement the strategy [3]. Moreover, the endorsement is expected to go beyond the project's lifetime for effective implementation, also considering key stakeholders' procedures for the participatory planning process.

Developing and testing health tourism products and service chains is a complex undertaking, in which industrial actors play the main role. However, since they are directly responsible for only a certain percentage of resource usage and related innovative cases, all actors have roles and responsibilities for the strategic development of nature-based health tourism (NHT). Therefore, it is essential to inform and involve stakeholders (municipalities, institutions, enterprises, civil society organizations, and communities) while improving harmonization among them [4]. This chapter describes the methodology identified and carried out in the HEALPS2 project to efficiently reach and engage stakeholders of Alpine NHT and to form a stakeholder group at the transnational level (including the engagement of EU-level actors and networks).

The key objectives are (1) to raise awareness of the complexity of developing NHT resource efficiency, and (2) to build common visions by harmonizing the interest of different players within the urban planning and environment conservation sectors. While the leading role may be taken by a variety of different members of the municipality, all stakeholders need to be involved, with clear individual responsibilities and roles in the process to ensure horizontal and vertical, as well as cross-sectoral cooperation between public authorities, local communities, and industrial players of Alpine destinations. A transnational and transversal approach is built on unique Alpine natural health resources and strengthens the Alpine territorial innovation capacity.

Key benefits identified in HEALPS2 with stakeholder group formation include:

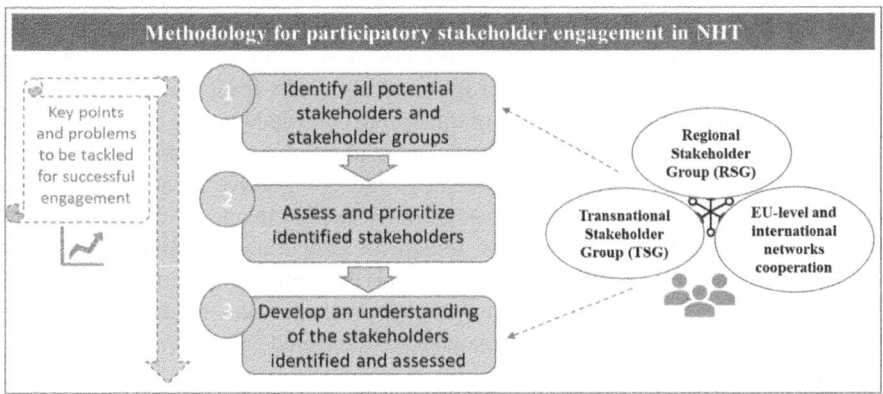

Fig. 1 HEALPS2 methodology for participatory stakeholder engagement

- investigation of issues from several perspectives;
- understanding local needs;
- better understanding and monitoring of the community perceptions;
- collecting and sharing ideas and good practices;
- networking, improvement of working relationships and gaining trust (these networks and new relations can also be used after the HEALPS 2 project end);
- assistance/advisement at the decision-making;
- achieving/ensuring more sustainable results;
- raising awareness of NHT as a tourism product and its positive effects in the local region;
- providing people and organizations with an opportunity for personal development through engagement activities;
- identifying effective dissemination avenues;
- using stakeholder meetings for marketing purposes (e.g. in press releases).

The following Fig. 1 details the steps and the key elements of the methodology for stakeholder engagement in NHT identified in the HEALPS2 project.

Specifically, the main process foresees the three steps below described.

2 The Process of Stakeholder Engagement and Endorsement in the HEALPS2 Project

In the planning phase of the stakeholder endorsement process, HEALPS2 partners bore in mind that there is no single best way to involve them. The various steps and decisions are greatly interlinked, considering the specific context, issues, and needs. Therefore, it has been framed as a repeating process, allowing several feedback points during progression.

The methodology adopted in the project is based on the Quadruple Helix concept [5]. Participatory engagement of representatives from each research and innovation sector in all project phases is essential for creating results from which all involved stakeholders can benefit. The benefits of quadruple helix stakeholder engagement by the development of collaborative networks are evident: they allow access to knowledge, development of scientific competence, and competitive advantage through the acceleration of ideas. Complex issues can be tackled thanks to the intersection between the areas of expertise and the search for cooperation in finding solutions between academics, industry, government and civil society or the citizens [6].

Having established clear reasons for engagement, the stakeholder engagement process in HEALPS2 involved three main steps, identified as follows.

2.1 Step 1: Identify All Potential Stakeholders and Stakeholder Groups

The identification of the stakeholders to be involved or consulted in the engagement process while finding the right mix of participants and ensuring that no group is unintentionally (or perhaps, deliberately) excluded, is essential to providing legitimacy and credibility to the engagement process.

In the context of public participation, a stakeholder can be defined as any person with an interest in the project or anyone that could be potentially affected by its delivery or outputs.

Potential NHT stakeholders are (if applicable to the single destination):

- national and local authorities, chambers
- local/regional hotel association, environmental groups, (national) park organization
- municipality workers and experts
- protected areas
- civil society organizations
- economic leaders, analysts, experts
- educational institutions
- industries, major companies
- transportation companies, public roads administration
- public utilities
- social institutions, consumer protection organizations
- health care organizations
- journalists, media contacts
- the broader lay public, residents, and young people.

These institutions, companies, organizations, and individuals should be mapped and contacted, and a short-written introduction of the project should be communicated to them, as well as the possibility for further participation. If the aim is to be inclusive and open to whoever wants to be involved, the best approach is often to identify an initial list of relevant stakeholders. In this first step, it is important to consider not only how they may be able to contribute to the project but also what will motivate them to become involved.

Although it is important to try to include all relevant stakeholders, it must be emphasized that it is not necessary to include them to the same extent. Not all stakeholders are equally interested in and affected by the project. The purposes of stakeholders can vary from getting information/data, technical or professional assistance, or just general contributions, to having the opportunity to express their concerns (which is usually the case with the broader civil society). Good planning defines the scope of engagement so that different people can be involved only in those parts of the process which are most relevant to them, and goals can be achieved in practice. Thus, it is useful to identify stakeholders by considering all aspects of the area of influence throughout the entire cycle.

Another key issue to be decided is whether the stakeholder identification is performed by the project team, or in collaboration with other colleagues, organizations, and cross-sectoral stakeholders. Possible ways to identify all stakeholders include:

- Consulting with colleagues to share knowledge about who may have an interest.
- Brainstorming with other organizations that have been involved in similar activities or those working on similar topics.
- Advertising, promoting the project and the engagement process (e.g. press releases about the project, leaflet, newsletter about the project, social media, website) and encouraging local organizations with an interest to come forward.
- Using 'snowball sampling' techniques: one stakeholder identifies further stakeholders until no additional new stakeholders are identified.
- Using existing partner networks: pre-existing networks are hugely valuable for beginning the process. It is one of the fastest and easiest ways of stakeholder involvement.
- Performing thematic research based on professional areas/disciplines included in the project.

All the suggested techniques are more effective if properly combined, considering their strengths and weaknesses. On the one hand, using the existing networks maybe lead to quickly coming results, but some key players could be missed because of being more active in other nature-based health disciplines or topics. On the other hand, desktop research and/or brainstorming can produce new stakeholder contacts but are not directly reachable.

Step 1 should result in a complex list of potential stakeholders from different levels. The following Step 2 foresees to assess, analyze and prioritize relevant stakeholders.

2.2 Step 2: Assess and Prioritize Identified Stakeholders

There are several ways of analyzing, grouping, or mapping stakeholders in literature. As anticipated, the Quadruple helix framework is one of the most adopted approaches to identify stakeholders by sectors and their roles in the project. Quadruple helix framework is based on collaboration between the public sector, academic sector, private sector, and civil society sector.

The approach foresees classifying stakeholders based on their relevance and significance to the project. Power mapping is a conceptual way of determining who needs to be influenced in the project, who can influence the project target results, and who can be influenced to promote the broad adaptation of the project results.

The HEALPS2 project categorized stakeholders by their relationship to the investigated topic or project outcomes. Specifically, three groups were identified:

1. Primary stakeholders—people/groups that are directly affected, either positively or negatively, by the actions of an agency, institution, or organization. In some cases, some primary stakeholders are oppositely affected: a regulation that benefits one group may harm another. A rent control policy, for example, benefits tenants but may hurt landlords.
2. Secondary stakeholders—people/groups that are indirectly affected, also either positively or negatively, by the actions of an agency, institution, or organization, but are not regularly engaged in transactions with the projects and may not be essential for projects survival.
3. Key stakeholders—might belong to either or none of the first two groups, they are those who can have a positive or negative effect on an effort, or who are important within or to an organization, agency, or institution engaged in an action.

HEALPS2 partners are committed to identifying not only the primary stakeholders in each of the Alpine regions but more specifically the key stakeholders and stakeholder groups from the NHT industry who will benefit from and therefore contribute and be engaged to the project's effort.

2.3 Step 3: Develop an Understanding of the Stakeholders Identified and Assessed

In a multi-stakeholder environment, it has to be considered that each stakeholder has its own set of goals and objectives and is often driven by a different set of needs. Often there are conflicting interests which could negatively affect the outcome of the engagement. Therefore, it is important to understand the perspectives of individual stakeholders and their relationships with each other when they are involved with planning and implementation.

Therefore, it is fundamental to understand the relevant stakeholders. Some key questions should be considered during this stage:

- Is there an existing relationship between the project and the stakeholder? Is there an existing relationship between the stakeholders?
- What knowledge do the different stakeholders have that may be relevant to the project?
- What views are the stakeholders likely to have about the project and its outcomes? Will these views be positive or negative?
- Is there a potential for any conflict amongst stakeholders? Or between stakeholders and the project?
- What are the appropriate means of communication? Will they need to be adapted to reach certain groups or individuals?
- Is there a willingness to engage? If not, why not and how could this be overcome?
- Are there any barriers to participation and engagement (e.g. technical, physical, linguistic, geographical, political, time, information or knowledge)?

The completion of the three steps should take into account different elements, including tackling specific problems, for successful stakeholder engagement. These are described below.

3 Elements to Be Considered Along the Stakeholder Engagement Process

3.1 Key Points for Successful Stakeholder Engagement

The HEALPS2 consortium identified some key elements that emerged from the project experience as pivotal to successfully engaging stakeholders. Once all three steps of the process are completed, the possibility to participate should be directly communicated to the identified stakeholders. The communication could be delivered via regular mail, e-mail, telephone, or in any other channels of accessibility, as well as publicized on websites, in local newspapers and on the notice board of the municipality. The information should contain the fundamental details of the project as well as the main stages of participation. It is fundamental to maintain clear aims for engaging the selected stakeholders in the project, beyond their benefits and motivations of stakeholders to be involved.

Every engagement process is different and needs to be properly funded and managed. Each partner should plan their engagement and adapt the process to suit the needs of both the project and the stakeholders alike.

To this aim, here are a few key points to successful engagements:

- engage in dialogue with stakeholders as equals and value their knowledge;
- allow stakeholders to help plan their engagement;
- use 'knowledge brokers' (who are connected to, and trusted by, different stakeholder groups) and experts in stakeholder engagement (including professional facilitators) if project teams do not have the expertise or experience;

- be prepared to be flexible and adaptable, tailoring project activities and communication of findings;
- ensure communication can be easily understood by all stakeholders—o not use complex or technical language unless this is asked for by the stakeholder;
- tailor engagement to the practical and cultural needs of stakeholders, bringing the project to where they are, at times of the day and year that are suitable for them;
- do not forget to provide feedback to stakeholders as soon as possible/promptly.

Factors like trust, openness, and commitment play an important role in working with the stakeholders. Once engagement has been achieved, it is important to maintain it by follow-up actions for a long-term, continued engagement. During the stakeholder activities, the following factors should be considered:

- Clarity—it is very important to clarify the objectives and goals of the engagement and to evaluate the appropriateness of the techniques.
- Management of information—stakeholders need to be persuaded of the benefits of sharing information. It may be necessary to present information in different ways as the attitudes and the way the information is processed by the stakeholders needs to be taken into account.
- Support and capacity development—the knowledge the stakeholders possess about the project varies depending on the different levels of their involvement. To enable them to contribute ideas and visions, each stakeholder needs to be on the same level of understanding as the rest of the stakeholders.
- Transparency—each stakeholder needs to be updated on the actions and opinions. They need to be assured that their concerns, requests, and expectations are addressed in a clear, open, and transparent manner.
- Trust-building—letting the stakeholders know that every stakeholder's view is valued and respected in the engagement process will give the assurance that their opinions are heard.

An example of the communication strategy adopted in the HEALPS2 project to inform and engage stakeholders is detailed in Chap. 8 [7].

3.2 Tackling Problems in Stakeholders Engagement

During the engagement process, the HEALPS2 project itself encountered some problems, which should be tackled proactively in a well-planned stakeholder engagement in the strategy-making process.

Many potential stakeholders could find low interest in cooperating at the meetings if they think their tasks are not important for the specific topic or strategy. Therefore, it is of utmost interest to create a positive background or a political will around them. The best way of this is a formal invitation by the mayor or the city council.

There might be opposite interests, like on economic terms, regarding aims and certain measures of the strategy/plan. This is a very good reason to conduct a proper stakeholder involvement: engaging stakeholders with opposite interests at an early stage in the process would help to get these problems promptly emerged, assessed and thus tackled.

A slow and erratic internal communication, or even the lack of it, leading to difficulties in reaching the right people, is a key problem to be considered. Communication problems could be mitigated by using more channels and means of communication, with dedicated time and efforts from the stakeholder manager.

The good use of channels and means of communication can be also important to avoid a low rate of participation and small attendance. Major societal actors should be addressed through their interests, valuable personal contacts, and efficient promotion.

Finally, involving too many stakeholders could slow down the strategy-making process. Utilize more groups with fewer people so that everyone may be heard and feels important—instead of overlooked—has shown success. If there are already existing groups, it is useful to leverage and organize their efforts and resources with a value-added approach. Conversely, if the groups themselves are poorly organized and utilized, they should be assisted in reorganizing or joining other groups.

4 Key Mechanisms for Stakeholder Engagement in NHT

4.1 Regional and Transnational Stakeholder Group

Throughout HEALPS2 project implementation, partners applied the stakeholders engagement process by involving target group representatives in Regional Stakeholders Groups (RSG). These groups were aimed at providing inputs to and feedback on HEALPS2 activities and outputs, with the participation in regular meetings at the local/regional level and the potential participation at interregional events. RSG meetings primarily contribute to the preparation and validation of the regional level outcomes with the engagement of RSG members in all activities, including some participation in interregional events.

In addition, the formation of the Transnational Stakeholders Group (TSG) helped to ensure, that organizations, regions and even institutions/networks outside the partnership learned about the possibilities offered by the tools developed as part of the project.

Based on prior relations and the contacts made during the proposal phase and the kick-off meeting, HEALPS2 partners mapped and approved the TSG members. The TSG was specifically aimed at involving representatives from territorial areas (also across the regions) that were not present in the consortium and had major experience in the exploitation of Alpine-specific natural healing resources, for the development of innovative tourism products and services chains.

TSG meetings primarily contribute to the validation of the regional-level outcomes and are interlinked with the RSG, with consultations and continuous feedback. Moreover, TSG members from countries with major progress in sustainable health tourism were invited to contribute with best practices and testing HEALPS2 solutions. Finally, the TSG can be used as an important vehicle to transfer the policy proposals and outputs to other regions and countries.

4.2 Engagement of EU-Level Actors and Cooperation with International Networks

One of the main activities in the HEALPS2 project was also the development of a concept for building a network of "Alpine Health Tourism Regions".

To this aim, it was fundamental to connect with the European networks in the field of nature-based tourism and healthcare (e.g. NECSTouR—Network of European Regions for a Sustainable and Competitive Tourism), attending relevant conferences, workshops, inviting international experts to the events of the project. Efforts made at soliciting inputs from all important actors in the local, national, and European fields (from professional organizations to business and policymaking), and embedding the project's results in European networks and policy frameworks, comprise an ongoing activity, complementing the joint strategy-building process. To achieve this aim, two major approaches were demonstrated valuable to be utilized:

> Participation as speakers in meetings, networking and professional events during the project implementation (e.g. participation at EUSALP Annual Forum, and other-EU thematic events, workshops, and conferences).
> Organization of public and invitation-based stakeholder events throughout the project (i.e. midterm workshop, final events, conferences), aimed at obtaining direct inputs and opinions from relevant stakeholders and networks.

5 Conclusions

This chapter presented the methodology adopted in HEALPS2 for participatory stakeholder engagement in NHT. The methodology integrates a process of stakeholder engagement and endorsement along three steps; the identification of the key points and the problems to be tackled for a successful stakeholder engagement; and the development of RSG and TSG that extend to the cooperation with EU-wide networks.

Developing health tourism products and service chains, and sustaining them with strategies and policies, is a complex undertaking. The adoption of the stakeholder engagement approaches throughout the HEALPS2 project showed that it is of utmost importance to properly identify, involve and communicate with the stakeholders who effectively complement the success of the project, and its outcomes, in enhancing NHT competitiveness. Factors like trust, openness, and commitment play an important role, together with the understanding of each stakeholder's view, especially when there could be conflicting interests. Thus, the strategy-making process should be framed as a repeating process, allowing several feedback points during progression, and with both RSG and TSG systematically contributing to the implementation and improvement of project outcomes.

References

1. E.T. Byrd, Stakeholders in sustainable tourism development and their roles: applying stakeholder theory to sustainable tourism development. Tourism Rev. **62**(2), 6–13 (2007)
2. V. Luyet, R. Schlaepfer, M.B. Parlange, A. Buttler, A framework to implement stakeholder participation in environmental projects. J. Environ. Manage. **111**, 213–219 (2012)
3. R. Stokes, Tourism strategy making: Insights to the events tourism domain. Tour. Manag. **29**(2), 252–262 (2008)
4. F.M.Y. Roxas, J.P.R. Rivera, E.L.M. Gutierrez, Mapping stakeholders' roles in governing sustainable tourism destinations. J. Hosp. Tour. Manag. **45**, 387–398 (2020)
5. E.G. Carayannis, D.F. Campbell, "Mode 3" and 'Quadruple Helix': toward a twenty-first century fractal innovation ecosystem. Int. J. Technol. Manag. **46**(3–4), 201–234 (2009)
6. A. Nigten, H. Kotey, Hybrid Learning environments: designing innovative, participatory and sustainable solutions for complex issues. Whitepaper (2017)
7. D. Spoladore, M. Geri, V. Widmann, Strategic communication in a transnational project—the Interreg Alpine Space project HEALPS2. in *Digital and Strategic Innovation for Alpine Health Tourism—Natural Resources, Digital Tools and Innovation Practices from HEALPS 2 Project*, ed. by D. Spoladore, E. Pessot, M. Sacco (Springer 2022)

Open Access This chapter is licensed under the terms of the Creative Commons Attribution 4.0 International License (http://creativecommons.org/licenses/by/4.0/), which permits use, sharing, adaptation, distribution and reproduction in any medium or format, as long as you give appropriate credit to the original author(s) and the source, provide a link to the Creative Commons license and indicate if changes were made.

The images or other third party material in this chapter are included in the chapter's Creative Commons license, unless indicated otherwise in a credit line to the material. If material is not included in the chapter's Creative Commons license and your intended use is not permitted by statutory regulation or exceeds the permitted use, you will need to obtain permission directly from the copyright holder.

Innovation Practices and Techniques for Nature-Based Health Tourism Competitiveness

Mirjana Nenad and Elena Pessot

Abstract Innovation is considered essential to the growth and long-term sustainability of health tourism companies and destinations. Continuous innovation takes place to improve the industry competitiveness, but especially the tourists' experience and wellness with new product offerings. This Chapter collects and describes the innovation practices proposed and developed in some pilot regions of the HEALPS2 project consortium. The innovation practices identified in the project can be subdivided into three types, i.e., innovation techniques, innovation supporting tools, and innovative product offerings. All the practices were designed to target several operators of the Nature-based Health Tourism (NHT) industry, from tourism facilities and companies (especially small- and medium-sized enterprises) to regional councils and municipalities in charge of policy-making and tourism strategy development. HEALPS 2 innovation practices and techniques can be purposefully integrated at the regional and local level for a more innovation-driven industry strategy and business development, as well as facilitation of transnational cooperation among key actors, also beyond Alpine regions and NHT destinations.

Keywords Health tourism · Innovation · Techniques · Tools

1 Introduction

1.1 The Pursuit of Innovation in Health Tourism

Despite the crisis initiated by the Covid-19 pandemic, tourism is still one of the most important and fastest-growing economic sectors at an international level. The lack of

---

M. Nenad (✉)
Scientific Research Centre Bistra Ptuj, Ptuj, Slovenia
e-mail: mirjana.nenad@bistra.si

E. Pessot
Institute of Intelligent Industrial Systems and Technologies for Advanced Manufacturing, National Research Council of Italy, Lecco, Italy

© The Authors 2023
D. Spoladore et al. (eds.), *Digital and Strategic Innovation for Alpine Health Tourism*, SpringerBriefs in Applied Sciences and Technology,
https://doi.org/10.1007/978-3-031-15457-7_7

tourists travelling had huge consequences on the overall tourism economy, including health tourism enterprises. Nevertheless, the relationship of these enterprises with the healthcare system provided some opportunities to continue operations, with the need to further promote innovation in this industry [1]. Health policies and tourism market trends are addressing the health tourism industry as one of the main pillars in the development of many regions and countries, as it promotes growth, creates jobs, attracts investment, and boosts exports [2].

Innovation is considered essential to the growth and long-term sustainability of tourism companies and destinations, with continuous innovation taking place to improve competitiveness, but especially the tourists' experience and safety with new product offerings. Industry stakeholders are under pressure to continuously deliver new offerings and provide more, faster, and bigger experiences to remain competitive. Yet, some stakeholders are still reluctant towards innovating their value offers, often due to the financial burden or the fear of possibly losing some authenticity in the healing treatments or activities, e.g. by radically changing the participant experience in a negative way [3].

Different means could be exploited to innovate the promotion of the true value and potentialities of natural resources in health tourism destinations [4]. At the same time, it is fundamental that tourism experiences remain "meaningful" to produce desired innovation potential. The notion of 'meaningful tourism experiences' herewith incorporates the values of the three generations of experience economy (i.e., staged experiences, co-creative experiences, transformative experiences) in fostering: (a) pleasurable and enjoyable experiences designed for many tourists; (b) personalized and extended interactions with the tourists and other tourist stakeholders; and (c) life-changing transformation for a few individuals [5]. In this sense, innovation initiatives in Nature-Based Health Tourism (NHT) destinations should integrate the engagement of all relevant stakeholders, and be addressed to implement holistic offerings that produce meaningful experiences of health, wellness and tourism.

1.2 Development of Innovation Practices in the HEALPS2 Project

This Chapter collects and describes the innovation practices developed by the HEALPS2 consortium, aimed at enhancing the attractiveness of health tourism opportunities in Alpine regions. All the practices were designed to target several operators of the NHT industry, i.e., tourism facilities and companies (especially small- and medium-sized enterprises); sectoral and specialized agencies such as destination management organizations, business support organizations, tourism organizations; regional councils and municipalities in charge of policy-making and tourism strategy development; but also universities and research centres. They reflect the requirements and needs of the specific areas, but they were formulated to be easily transferable into

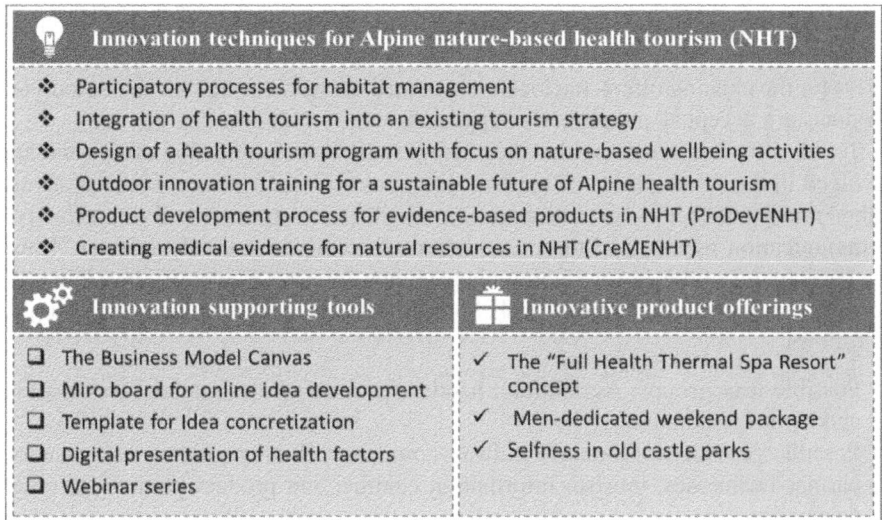

Fig. 1 Types of innovation practices identified in the HEALPS2 project to foster the competitiveness of the NHT industry

other regions and NHT destinations. In this case, a proper adaptation to local conditions should be considered in terms of existing infrastructure, level of engagement of local and regional stakeholders, needs and factors of tourists.

The innovation practices identified in the project can be subdivided into three types, i.e., innovation techniques, innovation supporting tools, and innovative product offerings (see Fig. 1). The three types, and in general the innovation practices presented, can be purposefully integrated at the regional and local level, according to the aims in terms of innovativeness and competitiveness of each NHT destination.

The three types of practices are described in the following sections.

2 Innovation Techniques for the Alpine NHT

2.1 Participatory Processes in Health Tourism Destinations: Cooperation Between Destinations and Municipalities in Habitat Management

This technique is developed starting from the awareness that NHT destinations are living spaces, where the relationship between guests and locals should be redefined. Decision-making processes of the actors directly involved in the tourism sector (hoteliers, tourism professionals, providers of tourism products such as hiking guides, producers of regional products, farmers, foresters, etc.) do not often include municipalities in the destination, which bring in the viewpoint of the population. As multipliers for the existing offers, the locals can contribute to ensuring that health tourism products are accepted and properly supported.

To this aim, it is necessary that they also benefit from the existing offers, and are involved in the development of tourism strategies with their policy representatives. Other important factors are transparency, which has to be ensured with effective communication means, and the presentation of results in a timely manner. Thus, the participatory process for Habitat management foresees to identify possible user groups, providers, local/regional stakeholders, and other interest groups or people, as follows:

- Possible user groups: Agriculture, handcraft, trade, clinics, nature conservation and alpine association.
- Possible providers: Mountain railway companies, hiking guides, trail owners, partner businesses, tourism information centres, and product partners of other destinations.
- Possible stakeholders: Municipalities (at administrative and political level), provincial governments, and civilian population (interested locals).

These groups can work effectively by discussing possible developments and joint actions in working groups and exchanging information several times in joint events. To this end, it is important ensuring that all possible stakeholders are invited to participate in the working groups. Moreover, cooperation with municipalities requires considering the laws, ordinances, and guidelines that bound their operations, thus proper municipal committees should be elected, and share decision-making with the mayor.

2.2 Integration of Health Tourism into an Existing Tourism Strategy

The regions that aim to develop NHT offers should firstly consider and include the existing tourism strategy, without disregarding it. The integration extends also to the existing natural resources, their current use and the tourism offers.

This innovation technique was applied in the Bregenzerwald region (Austria), where local tourism stakeholders were invited to a meeting to discuss all existing offers (without specifying the provider). These were properly clustered, and gaps in the potential health tourism offer were also defined. The latter included the availability of specific natural resources and facilities suitable for health tourism aims. For example, it emerged that the resources "forest" and "water" could be easily exploited for healing treatments, with many Kneipp facilities located in the forest or near a forest no longer used. In the next period, the team of Bregenzerwald Tourism is planning to develop and implement measures for the valorization of all Kneipp facilities, with their integration into existing offers and packages, without developing a completely new offer.

Also in this technique, the involvement of different stakeholders allows for creating a complete overview of the existing resources, services and infrastructure. Participative efforts are also required in the development of product offerings, and the integration into existing services, also to guarantee their acceptance in the existing strategies.

2.3 Design of a Health Tourism Program with a Focus on Nature-Based Wellbeing Activities

This innovation technique addresses regions where there is still no functional destination management, and a strategic approach for exploiting existing natural resources is missing. Specifically, it entails the creation of health and tourism programs focused on spending time in nature to enhance wellbeing, and on outdoor activities such as biking and hiking. The development of these programs includes a series of steps that are based on the existence of few initiatives, or even the lack of a strategic approach. Indeed, the steps to implement such a technique are:

- Analysis and evaluation of the quality and integration possibilities of the existing offer.
- Modelling of potential program content with suitability analysis.
- Preparation of basic material with a description of the program (content, logistics, integration).
- Examination of technical, logistical and organizational capacities in the region for the implementation of the program.
- Coordination between stakeholders and partners involved in the program.
- Preparation of information materials and communication content.
- Development of sustainable program management and marketing plan.

This innovation technique was applied in the region of Pomurje (Slovenia), where a functional destination management organization is missing. During the first step of the analysis, it emerged that the most important stakeholders to be involved in the program were the SMEs, such as incoming agencies, tourism and accommodation organizations, and tour guides. These were involved in all the subsequent steps, together with the public (visitors), sectoral agencies and local/regional authorities, and some prototypes of developed programs were evaluated for possible integration into existing offers of the destination.

2.4 Outdoor Innovation Training for a Sustainable Future of Alpine Health Tourism

This innovation technique foresees a two-day outdoor innovation workshop for health tourism stakeholders based in the Alpine region. The workshop was designed with the aim of training participants in entrepreneurial patterns and fostering idea generation and networking between different actors in the health tourism sector while spending time in nature. The idea is that experimenting with methods and exercises outdoors can be a catalyst for creativity, development of new ideas and innovative concepts for the development of the same region where the outdoor training takes place.

The training follows the principle of effectuation, based on entrepreneurial research that focuses on learning entrepreneurial thinking and acting through practical principles and an action-guiding process, thus overcoming the classic management approach of analysis-planning-goal setting-executing. It addresses the dynamic environments where a new logic for entrepreneurial behaviour is needed, by stimulating emergent responses that business actors are not able to plan.

This innovation technique was developed in the National Park Schwarzwald. Here participants practised the "ethics of reticence", with nature left to itself without human beings "planning" in which way nature should have developed. By letting nature develop on its own, participants could observe how new unforeseen things can happen that human beings would have been unable to plan. With the principle of effectuation, the actors from different European regions promoting NHT were able to reflect on the opportunity for a sustainable future for the overall health tourism industry. They firstly exchanged their experiences about the changes characterizing health tourism, i.e. the increasing awareness and consciousness of their health, lifestyle and new (mental) diseases (e.g. burn out); the demographic changes driving new needs of tourists travelling for wellbeing; the changes in service providers, with new networks, platforms and cooperation opportunities (e.g. hospitals corporate with tourism boards); the new frame conditions, with changes in the health care system, less support by health insurance, and more private/self-paid patients. Afterwards, they conceptualized new ideas for new offers as well as cooperation opportunities for potential joint future projects.

The workshop revealed to be particularly helpful to identify means to promote health tourism in the regions with the use of digital technologies, considering that during the first steps of a (digital) disruptive innovation the planning and analysis tools are not always adequate to take the next entrepreneurial steps.

The main features and outcomes of the innovation technique can be summarized as follows:

- Exchange of experiences between actors from the health tourism sector, by thinking and learning in nature and with heterogeneous groups of actors.
- Developing a common understanding of sustainable health tourism and joint criteria for sustainable health tourism, with the emergence and integration of different perspectives.

- Identifying new ideas and offers for the NHT sector that will be potentially implemented afterwards in cross-border consortia, and especially driving the adoption of digital technologies.
- Design and test an innovation workshop format that exclusively takes place in an outdoor environment where participants are (almost) continuously moving (e.g., hiking), with an enhancing effect on participants' creativity.

2.5 Product Development Process for Evidence-Based Products in NHT (ProDevENHT)

This innovation technique entails the basic path from the existence of a natural resource to the creation and use of medical evidence for the touristic valorization of the resource. So far, most health tourism offers lack a real link between tourism and medicine, with many offers in NHT that are not evidence-based. To develop high-quality and effective health tourism based on natural resources, the step to creating evidence is indispensable. In addition, both a regional and operational analysis of the framework conditions as well as the implementation potentials are necessary. In the proposed path, there is the possibility of integrating cross-sectoral services and offers into the tourism offer, especially in medical or health-oriented services, and establishing topics such as good nutrition and good sleep with local partners as a direct part of the tourism value chain. At the same time, this increases the potential of a broad regional anchoring and thus also acceptance of this type of tourism in the region.

The innovation technique entails a process of four structured steps that support interested stakeholders in creating medical evidence and subsequently using it for touristic valorization. The four steps are identified as (1) Assessment of Health tourism Potential and Customer Needs, (2) Medical Scientific Research, (3) Product Development and Implementation, and (4) Evaluation. As shown in Fig. 2, they should be realized in sequence with a continuous improvement approach, with the Evaluation phase providing inputs for the subsequent cycle.

The first phase foresees the identification and matching of the natural health resources and the at-risk population demands of a specific region. According to the content of the evidence gathered, results could differ from region to region. The second phase for the creation of medical evidence of alpine healing resources, with data analysis, requires the involvement and close cooperation of different stakeholders. Adequate resources should be planned for the search for and availability of suitable external partners (e.g. service providers or research institutes) that perform the clinical studies needed for the creation of the medical evidence.

The product development and implementation phase should leverage the knowledge from the analysis of existing case studies and consideration of potential market expectations; the definition of challenges in product development; the definition of requirements for education and training in health tourism; and the exploitation of adequate supporting technologies. Possible solutions are the cooperation of several

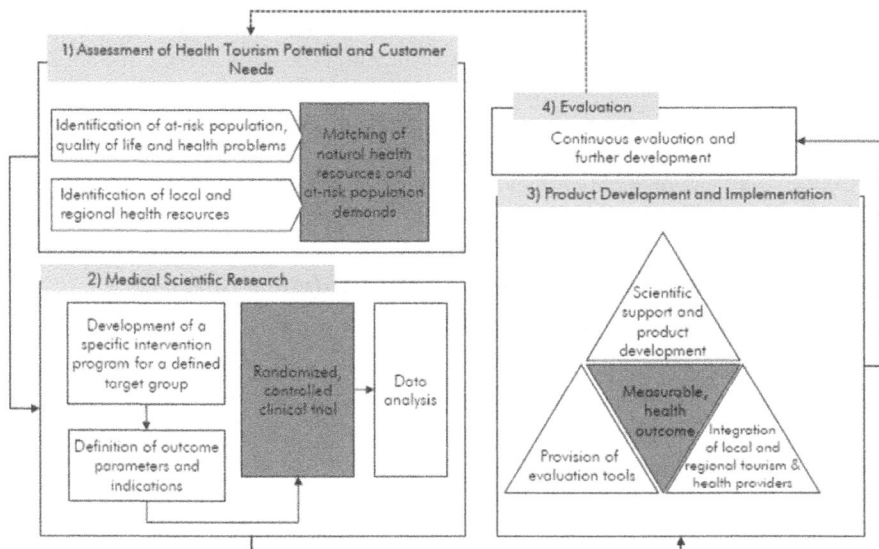

Fig. 2 Structural approach for the creation of medical evidence for natural resources

partners as well as a (co-) financing via subsidies, e.g., in the form of practice-oriented research projects such as the HEALPS2 project, where this innovation technique was first tested. However, if the process is completed and appropriate products are offered on the market at the end, the chance of creating a high-quality and regionally anchored product is very high. This type of NHT product development can therefore be properly evaluated to contribute to the overall sustainable development of a region.

2.6 Creating Medical Evidence for Natural Resources in NHT (CreMENHT)

This innovation technique extends Phase 2 of the Product development process for evidence-based products in NHT (ProDevENHT) described above with the basic path from the existence of a natural resource to the creation of medical evidence for its use within a nature-based and health-promoting tourism.

It is necessary to verify the effectiveness of the natural resources according to medical standards, to properly valorize them in NHT. The interaction between tourism and medicine considers the following elements:

- Health Tourism: location change and leisure setting are consecutive elements to distinguish health tourism from the use of local healthcare infrastructure and medical tourism.

- Indications: basis or rationale to use a certain NHT product.
- Evidence: evidence-based medicine means that decision-making on diagnosis and treatment is based on the best available current research, the physician's clinical expertise and the needs and preferences of the patient. Health-related interventions are based on the best available scientific research and integrate the clientele's interests, values and needs.

The innovation technique presented here shows stakeholders step-by-step how to create medical evidence for natural resources. The preparations up to the decision for a clinical study are very important since high costs are always associated and professional medical support is needed. The exact design of the clinical study is always individual and depends on the natural potentials as well as the objective to be defined and the budget. Anyway, the CreMENHT technique includes a list of general steps to create the evidence that can be easily and promptly applicable for NHT regions, i.e.:

1. Identify and evaluate existing natural resources for potential use in NHT
2. The decision for a clinical study
3. Definition of the objective of the study, with the formulation of the hypotheses to be investigated
4. Analyze existing case studies and consideration of potential market expectations
5. Definition of potential subjects, inclusion and exclusion criteria
6. Definition of the study procedure, determination of the measurement methods according to the defined objectives
7. Submission to an ethics committee application to conduct the study
8. Contracting trial insurance for the study
9. Implementation of the study on site
10. Evaluation of the study

This innovation practice extends the already existing studies that have demonstrated the effectiveness of natural resources, but that need to be integrated with further evidence. For example, positive health effects of green space are demonstrated for longevity, cardiovascular diseases, and mental health (see Chap. 1 [6]).

3 Innovation Supporting Tools for the Alpine NHT

3.1 The Business Model Canvas to Devise an Effective Business Model for New Local Wellness and Health Tourism Products

The Business Model Canvas is a visual framework adopted for the description, assessment, design, or improvement of business models. It can provide valid support for the development of new value offers—or extending the current offers—by including

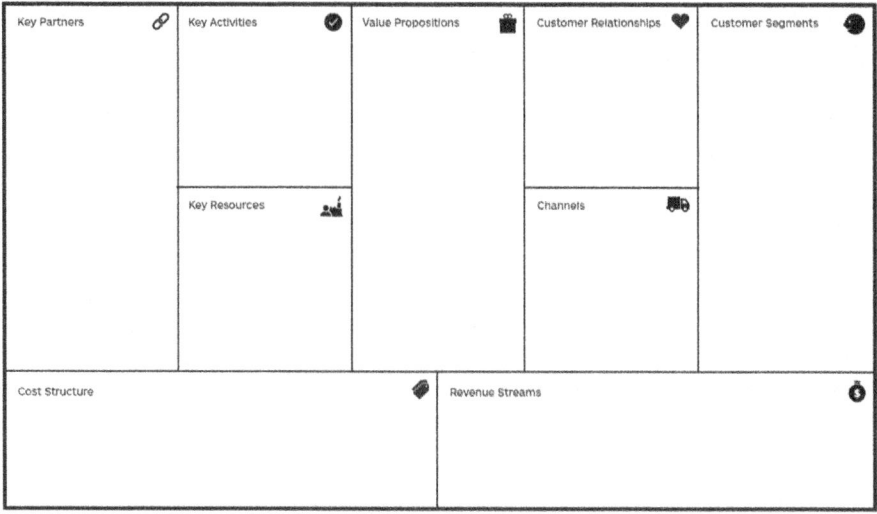

Fig. 3 The business model canvas template [7]

innovative wellness and health tourism products for the Alpine areas and positioning them as a relevant destination for wellness tourists.

The analysis takes into consideration nine blocks, grouped into the following four areas:

- infrastructure: including key partners, key activities, key resources
- offering: including value proposition
- customers: including customer relations, channels, customer segments
- finances: including cost structure, and revenue streams.

The template (Fig. 3) is filled in with concise qualitative information, aimed to facilitate brainstorming while not considering a quantitative assessment.

Usually, the business model canvas can be regarded as a preliminary step to the drafting of a business plan. It allows to schematically outline, in a way that is easy to understand even for non-experts, how businesses or other economic entities, create, deliver, and capture value. This tool can, thus, support the collective design of innovative business models of NHT within a participatory approach. The template can be printed out on a large surface so that groups of people can jointly start sketching and discussing business model elements with post-it notes or board markers. Thus, it represents a hands-on tool that fosters understanding, discussion, creativity, and analysis.

This technique was developed in a one-day workshop in the pilot area region of Ossola. This area is rich in resources which can effectively support the creation of a tourism offer focusing on wellness and health. At the same time, it has been observed that this offer is currently very limited. The main aim of this innovation technique was to involve the actors who could play a crucial role in the creation of new wellness and health tourism products in the thematic area, and a preliminary assessment of the viability of these initiatives. The target groups included local tourism businesses and professionals (and, in some specific cases, NGOs), together with local public administrations and institutions, which could support the development of the new products through their activities, projects and funding.

This technique can be very effective in comparing the different business models which can support the development of a specific new tourism product (e.g., visitors could be offered a program of guided hiking thanks to the financial support of the local government or hoteliers, or individual participants could be charged for each hike). The adoption of a participatory approach should consider the selection of stakeholders to be involved in the discussion: the group should not be too big so that each participant can effectively contribute, but at the same time not too small, to include different relevant points of view. Participants don't need to have specific economic skills but should have knowledge of the wellness and health tourism market and provide different perspectives. If this is not the case within the group of local stakeholders (as it happens when such an offer is still not developed in the area), such competencies should be guaranteed through the engagement of external experts.

3.2 Miro Board for Online Idea Development on NHT Products

The online collaborative whiteboard platform Miro (https://miro.com/) represents a valuable tool to foster innovation and development of health tourism product ideas based on the natural resources found in the Alpine regions. The Miro Board is initially designed to contain different categories of themes to be discussed. Stakeholders are provided with an example for each category and then asked to fill out the template with ideas on possible NHT products containing local natural resources, by writing them on digital post-its before allocating the ideas to one of the five categories. In the following steps, other stakeholders can further develop existing ideas by adding to the post-its and also bundle ideas. The main factor for developing the technique is that different stakeholders in every region would be interested in developing and offering NHT products but there is a lack of time and resources to come up with ideas on their own. Moreover, not all are aware of the local resources in the region and their level of evidence.

This innovation technique was employed in a workshop dedicated to the development of new NHT products for Val Müstair in Switzerland. The workshop consisted of three parts:

- Part 1: Generation of ideas for tourism products based on natural health resources
- Part 2: Concretization of the idea
- Part 3: Presentation of the results in the plenum.

In Part 1, all participants are asked to place their ideas for NHT in the region based on local resources. With this aim, the Miro Board consists of a template containing the five broad categories of food, water, agriculture, sports, and open categories. In the following step, participants were asked to vote on the best ideas generated and to prioritize and select 3 ideas for the next round. Specifically, these were: Trail running, the healing power of water & power sports, Detox-week (Fig. 4).

In the second part, the three ideas with the most votes received were presented again. After that, the participants were allowed to assign themselves to the idea they wanted to work on further. For this task, they had to answer the following questions: What is the idea concretely? Who would be the target group here? What is the need? What is the benefit of the idea for guests? Who could be the key players in this idea and what could the cooperation look like? A moderator from the project group made notes on a new Miro board.

In the last Part 3, one person per group had to present the idea shortly to the others. The workshop ended by asking the participants to join one of three action groups to further develop and implement the idea. In the following step, the ideas were defined in more detail. In effect, only one of the three ideas was developed into a product, while further brainstorming resulted in a separate idea, which had not been generated during the online workshop.

Miro is a tool that is easy to understand and adopt and does not require many resources. Once the Miro Board is created, it can be easily copied and applied to other regions, etc. Moreover, it represents a valuable technique to be used in the

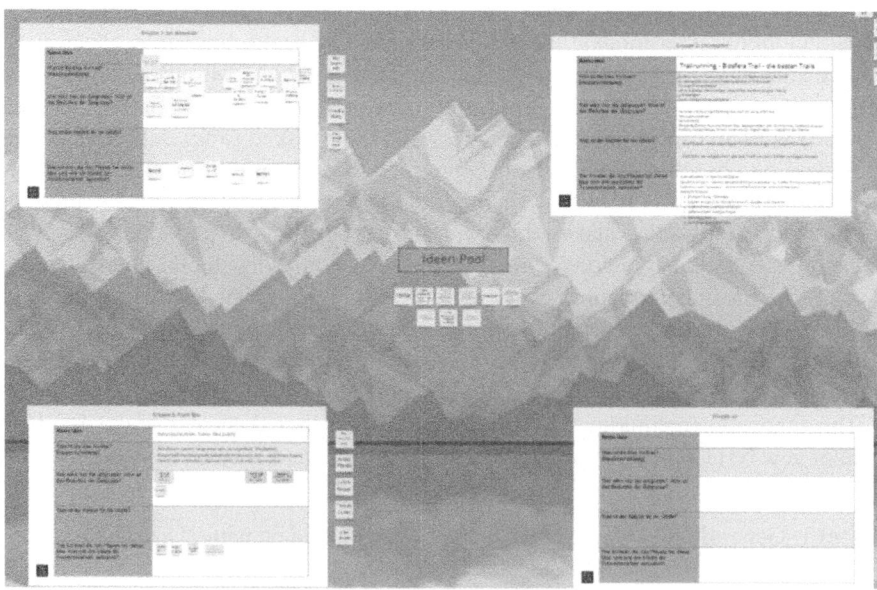

Fig. 4 Print screen of miro board with 3 developed ideas

context where physical interaction is not possible, as it was during the Covid-19 pandemic that prevented on-site workshops.

3.3 Template for Idea Concretization Within Alpine Health Tourism

This tool supports all the tools proposed in previous sections and adopted in workshops. The results and the ideas that emerged in these workshops should be further developed and concretized through a situation analysis. For example, an additional Part 4 of the workshop with the Miro Board (Sect. 3.2) should take place after the workshop, (asynchronous, or even individually). It should be dedicated to concretizing ideas by the researchers and interested parties and sharing them with the service provider. This concretization should include (desk) research to find out what offers are already available, who the competitors are in this area, what similar or identical offers already exist on the market and what the guests' needs are. A template with guiding questions to concretize the idea is thus designed as a key innovation technique of the HEALPS2 project, as follows.

Positioning/market potential (density of supply/demand trends).

- Are there intact natural and cultural landscapes?
- Are there special qualities or experience potential?
- What are the authentic/unique strengths of the region (experience potentials)?
- Which offers already exist, which do not?
- Is there already a thematic positioning locally or regionally?
- Gaps in the offer? What is missing?
- Comparable or exemplary offers in the region or abroad?
- Current trends and market developments at the domestic and international level?
- What is the local/regional tourism destination like? Which target groups are already being targeted?

Target group/needs

- What are the lifestyle and information habits of the target group to be addressed?
- Who should be addressed?
- What are the characteristics of this target group?

Offer description (draft)/service modules

- What should the offer look like and what should it contain?
- Who (service provider of the region) should play a part in the offer?

All these questions can help to grasp the idea in more detail and concretely develop it in a task force with the service provider. To concretize the idea, a collaboration platform can be used to work on the concept simultaneously, but this can also be done in a Word template and sent by email to other partners (research partners, service providers) for further comments on the concept.

3.4 Digital Presentation of Health Factors

The use of digital tools represents a valuable innovation for customers who are looking for NHT products and want to see how the product is working on them. Specifically, digitalization could enable visitors to visualize the effects of locations such as many Alpine regions, which are important energetic areas with healing effects, and make them "feel" their unique value. Specific tools can project an image or data of individuals' health components before and after the use of certain health products and offer an interactive insight into historical buildings or natural areas.

This issue allows health tourism destinations to tackle issues such as the fact that some historical remnants and natural areas are not approachable due to preservation demands.

3.5 Webinar Series to Foster Interest and Involvement of Local Stakeholders

This innovation supporting tool entails the organization of a series of webinars to stimulate a reflection on wellness and health tourism among local stakeholders and get in contact with local businesses and professionals which could potentially contribute to the development of the regional offer. The webinars should have a common thread, while a specific focus for each webinar should be identified. To guarantee broad participation of local stakeholders at multiple events, maximum flexibility should be ensured in the access to the contents. Thus, webinars are live-streamed, and the respective recordings remain available on various channels, to allow interested stakeholders who were unable to attend live to benefit from the content. In addition, it is important to limit the duration of each event. After the last webinar, all registered participants are asked to fill in a questionnaire, in which they could express their opinion on the different events and, most importantly, provide proposals or requests for further information related to the development of NHT. Further events could be organized in the following for a more extensive discussion of each specific topic, based on the feedback obtained through the final questionnaire or during the webinars (e.g. with a few minutes after the presentations given by the main speakers, to be reserved for questions and remarks from the attendees).

The use of webinars grew especially with COVID-related restrictions and precautions and the limited number of participants in the organization of live events. The use of this innovation technique in the HEALPS2 project was promoted by the Ossola area. A series of five seminars, to identify and discuss proposals and requests for NHT development with a common thread on mountains, was organized as follows:

- "TOURISM, MOUNTAINS and... HEALTH. Focus on: REGENERATIVE TOURISM"
- "TOURISM, MOUNTAINS and... THE WINE AND FOOD SECTOR"

- "TOURISM, MOUNTAINS and... WELLNESS. Focus on: MOUNTAIN-THERAPY"
- "TOURISM, MOUNTAINS and... ACCESSIBILITY. Focus on: MOUNTAIN TOURISM FOR ALL"
- "TOURISM, MOUNTAINS and... SPORT"

The main aim was to arouse curiosity and initiate contact with local stakeholders who could potentially be relevant to the development of the local offer in the field of NHT. To provide participants with a broad range of information coming from experts with a hands-on experience in the wellness tourism field, the potential of this type of tourism has been explored during the webinars thanks to the involvement of some stakeholders (e.g. restaurateurs and experts involved in the creation of a local supply chain for game meat), as well as academics and professionals who have studied and developed interesting experiences in other Italian mountain areas. The main target group was represented by local tourism businesses, professionals, and NGOs, which would play a key role in the creation of a local NHT offer, followed by local public administrations and institutions to support these offers, and university students who could dedicate research or professional activity to contribute to the establishment of Ossola as an NHT destination. The presented technique, together with the choice of online events, makes it easier to adapt it to different contexts and contents.

4 Innovative Product Offerings for the Alpine NHT

4.1 The "Full Health Thermal Spa Resort" concept

This innovative product was designed starting from the challenge of imagining the thermal spa resorts of tomorrow. Thermal spa resorts have two core activities: thermal medical care and leisure tourism. Some resort actors also established a new activity, coherent and specific, around Preventative Health, aimed at creating destinations that offer equipment, services and accommodation in a favourable thermal and touristic environment, with specifically designed preventative health products meeting customer expectations. This concept of "Full Health Thermal Resort" can enhance destination competitiveness as it has to differentiate factor the focus on preventative health in genuine life and holiday destination (town or village). To this end, the resort governance should prioritize the collaboration between all resort stakeholders, foster to fully share of the project's ambition and collectively aim at creating, developing, and achieving the Full Health Thermal Resort.

The innovative technique was developed in the Auvergne-Rhône-Alpes region (France) as part of the smart specialization S3 strategy initiated by the European Commission in 2014. The concept was formalized in a shared document, followed by the creation in 2015 of a "Full Health Thermal Resort" Blueprint elaboration methodological guide. Thus, the innovative technique is being implemented in the pilot resorts of Châtel-Guyon and La Bourboule and is included in the 2016–2021

4.2 Men-Dedicated Weekend Package

This innovative product was designed starting from the idea that several touristic products are mainly dedicated to women, with a lot of offers to choose from. Conversely, male tourists usually receive eventful products. The product ideated in the Spodnje Podravje region (Slovenia) develops a three-day weekend package reserved for men, including slow homemade food, slow wine tasting, and spa relaxation. The concept integrates the principles of Mithraism, an ancient religion reserved only for men, and the slow tourism concept.

The innovation technique collocates in a tourist product niche, with a lack of stress-relief products for men in the region. The new health tourism product can also align with other touristic offers—wine tasting, homemade food, spas, experiences in nature (walking, hiking, cycling, water sports)—and provide a value-adding offering to regions aiming to reach new market segments.

4.3 Selfness in Old Castle Parks

Different studies demonstrate that finding inner peace is an important factor in a healthy life. Selfness has become very popular in the concept of slow tourism, and many people are now embracing it. Selfness can be performed in many ways—walks, yoga, reading etc.—in peaceful outdoor places—forests, parks, mountains.

This innovative product is based on the importance of selfness, and the low availability of natural areas in urban contexts. It proposes the use of historical parks, and specifically, old castle parks, to be used for individual treatments. These parks are bigger than normal urban parks, they are beautifully structured, and often have some very rare flora and fauna in them. They also offer some insights into the history of the place, and all these factors combined make them a suitable place for some individual séances and therapies.

This health tourism product could be developed in two different ways: (1) with some instruction throughout the park (for example boards or instructions on the app) for solely alone experience, or (2) with a guide for individual treatments or small groups treatments.

5 Conclusions

This Chapter presented a series of innovation practices proposed and developed in some pilot regions during the HEALPS2 project. The innovation practices identified in the project were subdivided into three types, i.e., innovation techniques, innovation supporting tools, and innovative product offerings.

All the practices were designed to enhance the attractiveness of NHT opportunities in Alpine regions, but they were formulated to be easily transferable to other regions and health tourism destinations. To this aim, health tourism regions (or tourism destinations willing to integrate an NHT offer) should pursue a proper adaptation to local conditions in terms of existing infrastructure, level of engagement of local and regional stakeholders, and needs and factors of tourists. Each practice can be purposefully integrated into other practices, aiming for a more innovation-driven industry strategy and business development, as well as facilitation of transnational cooperation among key actors of the NHT industry. To this aim, it is useful the decision support system developed within the HEALPS2 project and illustrated in Chaps. 4 [8] and 5 [9].

References

1. R. Chirakranont, M. Sakdiyakorn, Conceptualizing meaningful tourism experiences: a case study of a small craft beer brewery in Thailand. J. Destin. Mark. Manag. **23**, 100691 (2022)
2. M. Hansen, A.M. Hjalager, A. Fyall, Adventure tourism innovation: Benefitting or hampering operations? J. Outdoor Recreat. Tour. **28**, 100253 (2019)
3. R.M.P. Medina, J.M.M. Martín, J.M.G. Martínez, P.S. Azevedo, Analysis of the role of innovation and efficiency in coastal destinations affected by tourism seasonality. J. Innov. Knowl. **7**(1), 100163 (2022)
4. E. Pessot, D. Spoladore, A. Zangiacomi, M. Sacco, Natural resources in health tourism: a systematic literature review. Sustainability **13**(5), 2661 (2021)
5. A.R. Szromek, The role of health resort enterprises in health prevention during the epidemic crisis caused by COVID-19. J. Open Innov Technol Market Complexity **7**(2), 133 (2021)
6. C. Pichler, A. Hartl, R. Weißböck-Erdheim, M. Bischof, Medical evidence of Alpine natural resources as a base for health tourism. in *Digital and Strategic Innovation for Alpine Health Tourism—Natural Re-sources, Digital Tools and Innovation Practices from HEALPS 2 Project*, ed. by D. Spoladore, E. Pessot, M. Sacco (Springer 2022)
7. A. Osterwalder, Y. Pigneur, Business model generation: a handbook for visionaries, game changers, and challengers, vol 1. (Wiley, New Jersey 2010)
8. D. Spoladore, E. Pessot, An ontology-based decision support system to foster innovation and competitiveness opportunities of health tourism destinations. in *Digital and Strategic Innovation for Alpine Health Tourism—Natural Resources, Digital Tools and Innovation Practices from HEALPS 2 Project*, ed. by D. Spoladore, E. Pessot, M. Sacco (Springer 2022)
9. A. Mahroo, D. Spoladore, P. Ferrandi, I. Lovato, A digital application for strategic development of health tourism destinations in *Digital and Strategic Innovation for Alpine Health Tourism - Natural Resources, Digital Tools and Innovation Practices from HEALPS 2 Project*, D. Spoladore, E. Pessot, M. Sacco (Springer 2022).

Open Access This chapter is licensed under the terms of the Creative Commons Attribution 4.0 International License (http://creativecommons.org/licenses/by/4.0/), which permits use, sharing, adaptation, distribution and reproduction in any medium or format, as long as you give appropriate credit to the original author(s) and the source, provide a link to the Creative Commons license and indicate if changes were made.

The images or other third party material in this chapter are included in the chapter's Creative Commons license, unless indicated otherwise in a credit line to the material. If material is not included in the chapter's Creative Commons license and your intended use is not permitted by statutory regulation or exceeds the permitted use, you will need to obtain permission directly from the copyright holder.

Strategic Communication in a Transnational Project—The Interreg Alpine Space Project HEALPS2

Daniele Spoladore, Marta Geri, and Veronika Widmann

Abstract Communication activities play a pivotal role in the management of research projects, especially those involving several partners and stakeholders from different countries. The Interreg Alpine Space HEALPS2 project relies on a transnational and transversal approach to improve the framework conditions and tools for alpine health tourism, and therefore proposes a communication strategy based on specific objectives. These objectives guide the communication activities at an internal and external level, with the latter being declined for different targets and stakeholders. In this Chapter, the communication activities are described, starting from the general and specific objectives-oriented approach, to the local realization. The general strategy and the analysis are illustrated, then are demonstrated through a regional use case—the Parco Regionale Alpe Veglia-Alpe Devero and Parco Regionale Alta Valle Antrona.

Keywords Project communication management · Communication management practices · Project management

1 Introduction

The overall objective of HEALPS2 is to develop and improve framework conditions and tools for a better use of Alpine-specific natural health resources for the development of innovative tourism products and service chains [1]. The project links

---

D. Spoladore (✉)
Institute of Intelligent Industrial Technologies and Systems for Advanced Manufacturing (STIIMA) National Research Council of Italy, Lecco, Italy
e-mail: daniele.spoladore@stiima.cnr.it

Department of Pure and Applied Sciences, Insubria University, Varese, Italy

M. Geri
Consultant of Aree Protette Dell'Ossola, Varzo, Italy

V. Widmann
ALPARC—Alpine Network for Protected Areas, Chambery, France

© The Author(s) 2023
D. Spoladore et al. (eds.), *Digital and Strategic Innovation for Alpine Health Tourism*, SpringerBriefs in Applied Sciences and Technology,
https://doi.org/10.1007/978-3-031-15457-7_8

academia, different business sectors such as the health sector, tourism and local service providers, as well as innovation and transfer agencies and protected areas to jointly implement new business models that improve value creation across sectors in Alpine regions. This transnational and transversal approach is built on unique Alpine natural health resources such as Alpine Water or Air Ions and strengthens the Alpine territorial innovation capacity. There are three specific project objectives (SPOs) the project works towards, which are defined in the project outline:

- SPO1—Increase awareness: Initiate mutual learning on health tourism development and implementation strategies from different regions by the involvement of actors from the quadruple helix (see Chap. 6 [2]);
- SPO2—Change attitude: Enhancing access to and use of innovation knowledge in Alpine regions regarding evidence-based health tourism development and cross-sectorial value chains;
- SPO3—Influence behaviour: Facilitate a more innovation-driven tourism policy and business development in Alpine regions.

All communication activities developed in the project build on the three project specific objectives as described above. Communication is a crucial element within the process of project implementation, having a transversal impact on internal and external processes. Hence, communication activities touch upon a multitude of internal processes, project management-related activities, but also on targeting the right stakeholders and efficiently disseminate project's results [3, 4]. Thus, communication is thematically relevant and results-oriented. Moreover, strategic communication shall build trust and establish reputation for the project success and its adoption on the local and regional level, leading to the long-term viability on the grounds.

However, strategic communication may only be successfully implemented if internal processes are well structured and organized: internal and external communication are closely intertwined and play both a role for determining project results' impact. *Internal communication* helps to coordinate the partnership for having a common basis of understanding, ensures activities cohesion and adds to capacity building among different stakeholders. Internal communication activities are addressed by the Management Work Package (WP) and the respective related handbook prepared by the Lead Partner of the HEALPS2 project, the Paracelsus Medical University of Salzburg. *External communication* supports the achievement of planned outputs by informing and actively involving target groups. It supports the dissemination of outputs and results to the large public and target groups not directly involved. These activities are structured within the communication strategy and coordinated by the Lead of the Communication Work Package ALPARC, the Alpine Network of Protected Areas.

The reminder of this Chapter is organized as follows: Sect. 2 introduces the communication goals, channels, and stakeholders to be addressed. Section 3 presents a SWOT analysis to identify opportunities and obstacles for a successful communication, then it presents the deriving communication strategy; Sect. 4 details the communications activities conducted and regional and local level, leveraging on the Ossola Protected Areas example. Finally, the Conclusions wrap-up the main outcomes of this Chapter.

2 Communication Goals and Channels

On the basis of the specific project objectives, the communication objectives increase knowledge, influence attitude and change behavior have been identified for the purpose of implementing the project outputs on the transnational level. For each of the three objectives, concrete measures and deliverables have been defined aiming at monitoring the working progress and the fulfilment of the different objectives.

In order to best achieve the three communication objectives, a stakeholder matrix [5] has been defined to identify key stakeholders and effectively target specific activities (Fig. 1):

The stakeholders constituting the targets to which address communication activities were divided in *Primary* (divided into internal and external) and *Secondary*. Project partners, subcontractors, financiers, Project Observers, and Alpine Space programme bodies, are included in the *Primary Internal stakeholders*, since they play a role within the project. Their needs and expectation can range from having the information to conduct an efficient cooperation (project partners), assessing intermediate and final project's results (financiers, Project Observers, Alpine Space programme bodies).

Primary External stakeholders encompasses public authorities at all levels (local, regional and national): they require clear and comprehensive strategic and management approaches, as well as tools, to support health tourism innovation factors. In this regard, many communication activities can be deployed at different level, ranging from involving these stakeholders in the project (by inviting them at key events, such as the mid-term and final conferences, providing the opportunities for networking events, inviting to capacity building trainings) to providing detailed information of

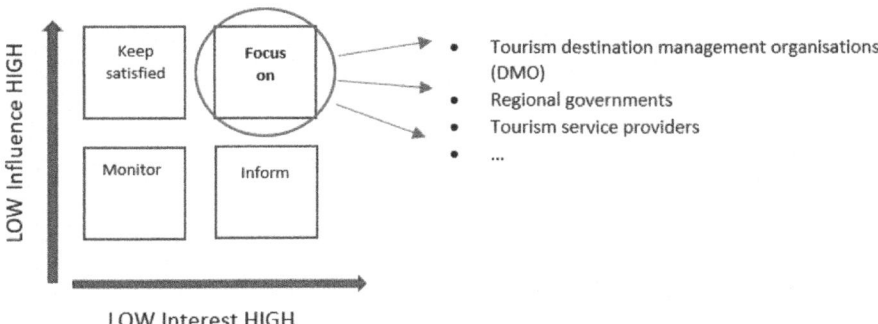

Fig. 1 The stakeholder matrix adopted for HEALPS 2

preliminary and final results. Sectorial agencies, Interest Groups (including non-governmental organizations) and international organization networks operating in the tourism sector fall in this category. Also, SMEs (hotels, cross-sectorial SMEs, etc.) and business support organizations relevant external stakeholders cover a pivotal role: they need to understand the project purposes and the value of its results to be properly engaged. Therefore, together with providing general and detailed information on any aspect of the project, these external stakeholders are also invited in mid-term and final conferences, as well as stakeholders' meetings. Finally, actors operating in the Education and Training sectors are also listed in this category.

The *Secondary stakeholders* includes local and regional media—in particular those of the areas in which HEALPS 2 pilot actions take place—and the General Public. For these stakeholders, transnational and local workshops and web-based communication are adopted to provide tangible information on HEALPS 2's ways to promote health tourism.

In a second step, operative communication guidelines have been defined to guarantee a coherent approach within the project consortium and adequately address the specific target groups. The basic communication package consisting of a project poster, flyer and roll-up provides for a common visual identity for all communication activities at different levels and adds to the visibility of the HEALPS2 results.

Moreover, several communication channels such as the project website, Facebook page and YouTube Channel are put in place to provide information and updates on a regular basis and foster every stakeholder involvement and results dissemination. The Facebook page is the main channel to inform on project progress, deliverables, outputs and crucial information related to the nature-based health tourism topic. YouTube is used for publishing videos produced in the course of the project such as official presentation clips but also testimonials and webinars organized by different project partners.

3 Communication Strategy for HEALPS2

The communication strategy for HEALPS 2 leverages on a SWOT analysis, which helps identifying the Strengths, Weaknesses, Opportunities and Threats relate to project communication.

3.1 SWOT Analysis for HEALPS 2

The SWOT analysis conducted for HEALPS 2 communication activities can be summarized as follows:

- Strengths: the research project leverages on a solid scientific approach, which can also make use of the findings and results of previous scientific research projects, as underlined in Chap. 1 [6]. Also, it provides concrete, applicable, scalable and tested results—e.g.: the shared knowledge model [7], the HTAB digital tool for tourism destinations [8], repeatable innovation techniques [9]. Moreover, the project partners composing the research team allow to cover for a multidisciplinary approach, which is required in a health tourism context. Considering the partners' distribution in the whole Alpine Space, the communication activities are able to cover different perspective—including sectorial, territorial and cultural ones—, as well as having an impact both at national and regional/local levels. Finally, the inclusion of representatives and relevant stakeholders within the project's Observer Partners helps in spreading the results toward a wider community.

- Weaknesses: the multidisciplinary approach may pose as a weakness, in that partners with different backgrounds and complexity may find challenging to understand findings and needs of other partners. Also, the different perspectives on health tourism need to be recomposed into the evidence and nature-based health tourism notion, basis of this project. Summarizing, the main weakness identified consists in "bringing everyone on the same page" before communication activities start.
- Opportunities: tourism stakeholders actively search for innovation and new markets; in particular, with the emergence of different forms of slow and sustainable tourism [10], stakeholders may be interested in the approach proposed by HEALPS 2. Also, the emerging health consciousness in the general public and the political willingness from investing in health (both at national and European levels) bode well for the core messages proposed by HEALPS 2.
- Threats: local-level stakeholders need to be engaged bearing in mind that they may not have all the knowledge necessary to apply the changes proposed by the project's results. Therefore, messages need to be carefully tailored. Also, as overtourism is a crucial factor for the natural ecosystem of Alpine Space, it is essential to stress the countermeasures deployed by HEALPS 2. Considering the general Covid-19 pandemic crisis, which might result in a large recession in the following years [11], it is essential to stress that investing in health tourism today may help local-level stakeholders to capitalize in the future.

With these coordinates in mind, the rest of this Section delves into the communication approach for the transnational level of the project.

3.2 Communication at the Transnational Level

Following the definition of internal processes for communication actions, the links to international and transnational institutions need to be established in order to favor respective synergies, enlarging the network on Alpine Health Tourism and strengthening the cooperation with institutional and political actors to improve the framework conditions for the positioning of Alpine Health Tourism.

The EU-Strategy for the Alpine Region (EUSALP) and the Alpine Convention are both multinational initiatives striving for sustainable development in the Alps and are therefore important addressees at the strategic policy level. A particular focus has been placed on achieving an active exchange with the Action Group 2 and Action Group 6 of the EUSALP. Moreover, two project partners are active observers of the Alpine Convention and assure the information flows for contracting parties. Further exchange and cross fertilizing are foreseen with similar Alpine Space projects, working in the fields of ICT based innovation and regional development. Examples for this communication are the ASP projects BifocALPS, DesAlps or AlpBioEco. During project lifetime other synergies to EU projects shall be detected and nourished.

Moreover, at policy level, addressing representatives of the EU Commission in particular from DG Regio is considered to help elevating the approach at the transnational strategic level. Moreover, ArgeAlp and cross border cooperation such as Euregios are addressed in the project lifetime e.g. at the HEALPS2 mid-term conference to increase the visibility of project results.

For the aim of providing a long-term knowledge base for the newly created network on Alpine Health Tourism, Innovation Salzburg and Paracelsus Medical University run the platform Healing Power of the Alps. This platform aims at supporting destination managers and interested regions in developing nature-based health tourism offers and informing interested stakeholders on latest scientific findings and developments in that sector.

In the next section, a thorough overview on the communication activities at the local and regional level are shown by referring to the example of the Ossola Protected Areas, project partner and pilot region in the HEALPS2 project.

4 Communication at Regional Level

The Ossola Protected Areas are two regional parks in Piedmont (North-Western Italy): Parco Regionale Alpe Veglia-Alpe Devero and Parco Regionale Alta Valle Antrona. For these two parks, the Ossola Protected Areas Management Authority identified new possible health tourism products using techniques of stakeholder involvement, such as webinars to illustrate innovations and options for new tourism value chains, and online workshops and events to meet, brainstorm and co-create a shared tourism development path. Ossola focused on the widespread psychological distress resulting from city life, whose figures further increased due to the pandemic [12]. The product that was then developed and tested through pilot events is the *adventure therapy weekend*. Adventure therapy is an outdoor-based approach aimed at increasing one's psychological wellbeing, by undertaking subjectively challenging activities in nature together with a group of people and then reflecting on each one's emotions and coping behaviors, to gain awareness and become able to use them in everyday life.

4.1 Objectives and Target Groups

The communication of the Ossola Protected Areas Managing Authority as a partner of the HEALPS2 project helped to reach the project regional strategic communication objectives through both the project official channels and partner channels. To communicate the activities carried out within the project, Ossola started identifying the priority target groups and by setting specific goals for each one. The priority target groups are the following ones:

- Local stakeholders: the Ossola Protected Areas Management Authority focused particularly on mountain guides, local businesses especially in the tourism and agricultural sectors and public authorities such as municipalities.
- Public authorities and associations at the regional, national, EU levels: this target group comprises a variety of higher level public authorities like the tourist and environment departments of the Piedmont Region, the Italian relevant ministries, the supranational EU strategy EUSALP, CIPRA international, the Alpine Convention and the European Commission.
- Other protected areas: national and regional parks in Italy and Europe, other protected areas. These were reached also through relations with the Alpine Association of Protected Areas ALPARC and with the European Federation of Parks Europarc.
- Tourists: this group includes both the tourists who already know and visit Ossola and those who are potentially interested but have never been in the area or don't even recognize it as a suitable destination. The focus on health and wellbeing has led the Ossola Protected Areas to widen the scope of communication beyond their traditional tourists (families and people who love mountains and outdoor sports), also to people who would consider a mountain destination provided it has a health tourism offer.

The SPO1 *Increase Awareness* was applied to four specific subjects:

(1) HEALPS2 Project and Ossola Protected Areas Management Authority. Making local stakeholders and authorities at regional, national and EU level aware of the existence of the project and of Ossola's role within HEALPS2 served as a first branding step.
(2) Nature-based health tourism potential and best practices. Showing what resources could be leveraged and what advantages health tourism would bring was essential in order to lead local businesses and administrators to consider the creation of new, health-related tourism value chains as a valuable option.
(3) Health benefits of nature. These are the reasons behind the choice to make a tourism product starting from some elements of the Alpine environment, e.g. a waterfall or a forest. They may also become a motivation for health-conscious people to spend more time in nature, including when they travel.
(4) Ossola nature-based health resources. Ossola is home to a variety of Alpine environments and is rich in natural resources for health and wellbeing. However, both practitioners and tourists aren't used to considering them as such. Raising

awareness about Ossola's many health natural resources helps positioning the whole Protected Area as a health-friendly tourism destination.

The SPO2 *Change Attitude* focused on:

(1) Arousing interest, curiosity, willingness to visit Ossola as a tourism destination focusing on health and wellbeing: Ossola communication was not limited to informing people about the health tourism natural resources the Protect Areas offer, but it also aimed at making such an offer desirable for the potential customers.
(2) Building the brand image of HEALPS2 Project and of the Ossola Protected Areas Management Authority. The communication carried out by Ossola as a project partner both contributed to building its own image as an health tourism actor and as an institution, and to highlighting the milestones the project reached.

The SPO3 *Influence Behavior* aimed at:

(1) Getting local businesses to work together as a network to co-design new tourism value chains for Ossola.
(2) Leading people to participate in the "adventure therapy weekend" pilot events, as part of the test of the viability and market acceptance of this idea.

4.2 Local Communication Activities

To reach the project and Ossola Protected Areas Management Authority branding goals, including awareness and attitude building, the partner used both the project and its own media. The project channels were used to communicate the partner's actions within HEALPS2 to an international audience, while also highlighting the project achievements. On the other hand, the main project events and results were highlighted through Ossola's corporate communication channels (website, newsletter, social media, press relations) and by sharing the project experience when participating in conferences, workshops and other events. To involve local stakeholders and start participatory processes aimed at co-designing a new tourism offer, it was necessary to raise awareness about the nature-based health resources Ossola offers and how they can be sustainably used to create a new tourist offer aimed at personal wellbeing. Communication on the Ossola Protected Areas channels and stakeholder meetings were essential to reach these goals.

Web. News on the Ossola Protected Areas official website and newsletter informed local stakeholders and followers about project activities, events and results; Facebook helped increase their awareness of the potential of nature-based health tourism, while Facebook and Instagram posts highlighted Ossola's nature-based health resources. The tourists were engaged through social media. Since, in Italy, spas are often seen as the only expression of a tourism aimed at being well, communication had to start by widening this concept to include also other natural resources and experiences that may turn a trip into a source of physical and mental health. The Facebook and

Instagram posts about the health effects of mountain activities, often mirroring the project "resource of the month" communication, were a first step in this direction. Then, the Ossola Protected Areas communicated the region as a destination focusing on wellbeing at several different levels with posts on Facebook and Instagram. To do so, they suggested ways to enjoy the health benefits of Ossola's health resources while highlighting the relevant tourist offer already in place: trails, itineraries, facilities, events, farms and local food producers. Also, this was a way to strengthen the relationship with local players and start building on possible synergies (Fig. 2).

During the three years of the project about 100 Facebook posts and more than 50 Instagram posts were published, and 9 newsletters containing articles about project activities.

Press and local workshops. Press releases allowed communication of news about project activities to a wider circle of stakeholders, at the local and regional level. The local players who had already started a closer relationship with the park (by adhering to the European Charter of Sustainable Tourism in Protected Areas) were reached through one-to-one contacts and through the invitation to local workshops and to transnational project events. The choice to focus on this subset of stakeholders as privileged partners comes from the idea that sharing the values of sustainability is crucial for the tourism innovation process in a protected area.

Results. The communication activities described above reached their goals. Up to 13 local stakeholders took part in the online workshops organized by the Ossola Protected Areas Management Authority, 110 people were involved in the four webinars; 25 local businesses took part in the day-long event organized on February 4th

Fig. 2 An Instagram post to promote the adventure therapy weekend tourism product

2022 and showed interest in coming together to build new tourism products focusing on wellbeing.

Hundreds of international stakeholders, protected areas and public bodies learnt about Ossola's activities in the project thanks to the participation of Ossola Protected Areas representatives as speakers in international online and in-presence events.

5 Conclusions

This Chapter drafts the strategic communication activities for the HEALPS 2 project. Starting from the identification of Specific Objectives, the Chapters delves into a the communication goals and stakeholders. A SWOT analysis helps surveying those project's aspects that can be leveraged to deliver efficient communication, and supports in recognizing criticalities that may require to be specifically address. Also, the Chapter dedicates considerable attention to local and regional development of communication activities, proposing the example from Ossola Protected Areas, delving into the detail and discussion of the communication activities conducted at a local level.

References

1. D. Spoladore, E. Pessot, M. Sacco, A. Hartl, C. Pichler, Preface. in *Digital and Strategic Innovation for Alpine Health Tourism* (Springer 2022)
2. D. Čeh, M. Nenad, E. Pessot, A methodology for participatory stakeholder engagement in nature-based health tourism. in *Digital and Strategic Innovation for Al-pine Health Tourism - Natural Resources, Digital Tools and Innovation Practices from HEALPS 2 Project*, ed by D. Spoladore, E. Pessot, M. Sacco (Springer 2023)
3. J. Falkheimer, The power of strategic communication in organizational development. Int. J. Qual. Serv. Sci. (2014)
4. K. Muszynska, K. Dermol, V. Trunk, A. DHakovic, G. Smrkolj, Communication management in project teams–practices and patterns. in *Joint International Conference* (2015), pp. 1359–1366
5. M.J. Polonsky, Stakeholder management and the stakeholder matrix: potential strategic marketing tools. J. Market Focus. Manag. **1**, 209–229 (1996)
6. C. Pichler, A. Hartl, R. Weisböck-Erdheim, M. Bischof, Medical evidence of Alpine natural resources as a base for health tourism. in *Digital and Strategic Innovation for Al-pine Health Tourism—Natural Resources, Digital Tools and Innovation Practices from HEALPS 2 Project*, ed. by D. Spoladore, E. Pessot, M. Sacco (Springer 2023)
7. D. Spoladore, E. Pessot, An ontology-based decision support system to foster economic and competitiveness opportunities of health tourism destinations. in *Digital and Strategic Innovation for Alpine Health Tourism.* (Springer 2022)
8. A. Mahroo, D. Spoladore, P. Ferrandi, I. Lovato, A digital application for strategic development of health tourism destinations. in: *Digital and Strategic Innovation for Al-pine Health Tourism—Natural Resources, Digital Tools and Innovation Practices from HEALPS 2 Project*, ed. by D. Spoladore, E. Pessot, M. Sacco (Springer 2023)

9. M. Nenad, E. Pessot, Innovation practices and techniques for health tourism competitiveness. in *Digital and Strategic Innovation for Alpine Health Tourism—Natural Resources, Digital Tools and Innovation Practices from HEALPS 2 Project*, ed. by D. Spoladore, E. Pessot, M. Sacco (Springer 2023)
10. E. Pessot, D. Spoladore, A. Zangiacomi, M. Sacco, Natural resources in health tourism: a systematic literature review. Sustainability **13**, 2661 (2021)
11. v Aldao, D. Blasco, M.P. Espallar-gas, S.P. Rubio, Modelling the crisis management and impacts of twenty-first century disruptive events in tourism: the case of the COVID-19 pandemic. Tourism Rev. (2021)
12. C.H. Vinkers, T. van Amelsvoort, J.I. Bisson, I. Branchi, J.F. Cryan, K. Domschke, O.D. Howes, M. Manchia, L. Pinto, D. de Quervain et al., Stress resilience during the coronavirus pandemic. European Neuropsychopharmacology **35**, 12–16 (2020)

Open Access This chapter is licensed under the terms of the Creative Commons Attribution 4.0 International License (http://creativecommons.org/licenses/by/4.0/), which permits use, sharing, adaptation, distribution and reproduction in any medium or format, as long as you give appropriate credit to the original author(s) and the source, provide a link to the Creative Commons license and indicate if changes were made.

The images or other third party material in this chapter are included in the chapter's Creative Commons license, unless indicated otherwise in a credit line to the material. If material is not included in the chapter's Creative Commons license and your intended use is not permitted by statutory regulation or exceeds the permitted use, you will need to obtain permission directly from the copyright holder.

Conclusion

The aim of this book was to present and discuss a set of strategies, practices and hands-on tools developed within the HEALPS 2 project to improve the framework conditions for a holistic growth of nature-based health tourism industry in the Alpine regions. The developed results are aimed at a better exploitation of Alpine-specific natural resources within innovative product and service offerings and collaborative value chains. Alpine tourism destinations can leverage resources such as thermal waters, clean air, or a peculiar microclimate to promote health tourism and enhance the local and regional economy. We considered all natural resources encompassing the destination physical features (i.e., mountains, lakes, rivers, forests) and also their related by-products (such as local food and remedies), together with their traditional cultures and heritage that characterize the Alpine regions.

Findings of the book derive from the integration of different methodologies and activities performed along the project duration. A review of scientific and grey literature on natural resources and their healing effects, and the innovation management issues in health tourism, was performed. The existing regional health tourism policies and ongoing projects were also evaluated, with evidence of specific needs and strategic success factors. The emerging themes were thus enriched with the data collected in the case studies performed in the pilot regions of the project and in focus groups with industry experts, policy makers and researchers on topics related to nature-based health tourism. The overall methodological framework built on a collaborative approach that allowed to engage since the beginning the plurality of stakeholders that characterizes the health tourism industry.

The combination of different methodologies resulted also in the implementation of different solutions, to be properly integrated for enhancing the overall industry competitiveness and sustainability. In this sense, a strategic approach for nature-based health tourism in Alpine regions should integrate the key base knowledge on medical evidence of healing effects and the perceptions of tourists; the innovative applications to assess regional KPIs and to support strategic decision-making to exploit local and

© The Editor(s) (if applicable) and The Author(s) 2023
D. Spoladore et al. (eds.), *Digital and Strategic Innovation for Alpine Health Tourism*, SpringerBriefs in Applied Sciences and Technology,
https://doi.org/10.1007/978-3-031-15457-7

regional natural assets; the innovation practices to be enriched by a quadruple helix approach to properly engage and enhance collaboration between stakeholders.

These results represent an important reference framework to guide industry operators in implementing strategies and techniques and enhance the capacity of Alpine regions to develop and implement innovative health tourism value chains with a collaborative, transnational approach. The integrated results will be finally collected into an Alpine nature-based health tourism Action Plan, including a set of recommendations for different policy levels as well as implementation toolkits for enhancing integrated value chains, and contributing to the positioning of the Alpine Space and its resources as globally attractive health promoting place.

The manufacturer's authorised representative in the EU is Springer Nature Customer Service Centre GmbH, Europaplatz 3, 69115 Heidelberg, Germany. If you have any concerns regarding our products, please contact ProductSafety@springernature.com

Printed and bound by CPI Group (UK) Ltd, Croydon, CR0 4YY

25/03/2026

02078172-0019